PARENT LIKE A TRIPLET

The Definitive Guide for Parents of

Twins and Triplets...

from an Identical Triplet

KARI ERTRESVÅG

Dedication

To all parents of multiples:

You got this!

Praise for Parent like a Triplet

Written by an identical triplet, *Parent like a Triplet* provides valuable insight to life growing up as an identical multiple. I would recommend it as a must-read for parents and parents-to-be of multiples. Keep a copy on the bookshelf, because you will find yourself going back to it many times as your multiples grow and develop into adults. As a parent of identical twins, I could relate to so much of what Kari has written. I only wish I had been able to use this book to guide my parenting years.

– Monica Rankin, Chairperson, The International Council of Multiple Birth Organisations

It's not often you learn something whilst feeling like you are having so much fun, but this book hits the spot. I'm sure lots of parents and multiples alike will get something from the highly entertaining stories within.

– Keith Reed, CEO, Twins Trust, UK

I loved every word! *Parent like a Triplet* is the 'bible' I have been missing. An honest, heartfelt, positive and uplifting book about life as a multiple that will change how you parent your twins or triplets.

– Sandra Moberg Ryan, mother of identical triplets, Sweden/Ireland

Kari Ertresvåg draws from a number of perspectives—including her own personal experience as an identical triplet, academic research by experts in the field of twin studies and studies of multiples, and conversations with her family members—to educate others about what life is *really* like as a multiple. She provides practical advice for parents on what to do/not to do when it comes to raising multiples such as encouraging one-on-one time and encouraging each twin or triplet to have their own friends, with the end goal of making life easier for young twins and triplets and ultimately as adults. Written with just the right amount of humor and the interwoven personal anecdotes, *Parent like a Triplet* is a must-read for new parents of twins and triplets.

– Joleen Greenwood, Ph.D., family sociologist, identical twin, and author of *Identical Twins: Adult Reflections on the Twinship Experience*

Loved it. So easy to read, informative, yet touching and funny. Reading Kari's book was, at times, like having a conversation with an old friend. Her honest and often hilarious anecdotes and stories are of growing up, and also go through the psychology as a multiple, and are backed up with academic studies and relevant data. But the real beauty in Kari's words are her snippets of actual events throughout her life, and how these helped carve out her own experiences and those of her family.

– Kirsty Saxon, Magazine Editor – *Multiple Matters*, Multiples NZ

What a delightful read! *Parent like a Triplet* offers invaluable insight into what it is like to grow up as an identical multiple. In addition to charming anecdotes, Kari Ertresvåg gives parents of twins and triplets on-point and practical parenting advice that will help them navigate various challenges that arise in families with multiples.

– Dara Lovitz, mother of fraternal twins and author of *Twinsight: A Guide to Raising Emotionally Healthy Twins with Advice from the Experts (Academics) and the REAL Experts (Twins)*, USA

This ground-breaking book fills a niche not only for multiples and parents themselves, but also for the professionals who look after them, including teachers. An extraordinary exposé from inside the multiple birth experience of how individuality and self-expression find their way despite the collectivism of being a twin or, in this case, a triplet.

– Lynda P. Haddon, Multiple Birth Educator and mother of fraternal twins, Canada

I am delighted that my work and that of other eminent researchers has been drawn upon to enhance the message of *Parent like a Triplet*. This book gives a unique perspective as it is written by an identical triplet. There is no-one better qualified to highlight that being a multiple is a special aspect of humanity that requires special understanding. Important issues are discussed particularly with reference to enabling each child to develop as an individual. Understanding things from the child's perspective helps us to make adjustments to meet their needs. Thank you for enabling parents, teachers, educators, health professionals and all those interested in multiples to benefit from sharing your unique experience.

– Pat Preedy, Ph.D., Honorary Educational Research Consultant for
Twins Trust, UK

A multiple parents bible to come back to again and again! The insight that Kari's book provides is unlike any dry textbook you get handed in the doctor's office when you first see the multiple flutters of heartbeats.

– Elly Turner, mother of identical triplets, Australia

This book will be invaluable to parents of multiples. I am so excited to learn from Kari's experiences so that I can then apply them to my own role as a mother.

– Kelli Kalvesmaki Ratliff, mother of identical triplets, USA

As a mom of identical triplet girls and an older son, I couldn't get enough of this book. Kari discussed many topics that my husband and I have discussed numerous times, e.g. should we put our girls in the same class in elementary school, and what it is really like being the older brother of triplets? This book is a must read for any parent of multiples, especially identicals. Thank you, Kari, for opening our eyes and allowing us to learn from your experience and for sharing interesting facts about twins and triplets.

– Lindsey Lafferty, mother of identical triplets, USA

Contents

Foreword

I consider myself Kari Ertresvåg's partner in crime—the "crime" being our joint commitment to debunking the *twin mystique* and normalizing the experiences of multiples. We share a sisterhood of sorts as fellow identical multiples—Kari is a triplet and I a twin. Although almost four decades separate us chronologically, we are emotionally and psychologically on the same page when it comes to our shared mission. Kari's extraordinary book is both a memoir and exposé, elucidating the blessings as well as the drawbacks of growing up as a multiple. *Parent like a Triplet* is deftly written with humor, authenticity, humanity, and insight.

What I most admire is Kari's uncanny ability to communicate the challenges of being a multiple from a childhood perspective. Her beautifully descriptive accounts of growing up with her two sisters are both comical and sobering. She does not sugarcoat the difficulties nor minimize the joys. Her recollections of growing up as a triplet are admirably candid and genuine. Though she decries society's romanticized, idealized view of multiples, she is delighted and excited to share her feelings about the incredible bond she enjoys with her sisters.

I particularly enjoyed Kari's thoughts on "taking pauses." Rather than using the words *separation* or *alone time*, she explains how taking pauses whenever possible with each individual child is an essential parenting task. Kari recounts how she cherished private conversations and one-on-one time with her mother. Though she is sympathetic about the challenges her parents faced in raising five children—three of whom were the same age—she reflects that a pause now and then would have done much to fulfill her yearning to be known and recognized.

Kari gives her readers specific advice and tangible strategies for meeting this longing for uniqueness and overcoming the many obstacles that prevent its healthy formation. For example, she explains that focusing on minor differences to differentiate between multiples can have unintended consequences that can last a lifetime and dangerously impede the emotional well-being of multiples as they mature.

I also admire Kari's willingness to tackle the thornier, less well-known issues that arise when raising multiples, such as the impact of sharing friends with siblings, how twins and triplets can deal with bullying, and why research findings about multiples that do not account for nuance and context should be taken with a grain of salt. For instance, she takes issue with the most recent statistics that indicate separating or keeping multiples together at school has no real impact on their development. Lumping these children into a percentage does not do justice to the individual experiences of twins or triplets in various circumstances.

Kari's basic message is akin to mine—parents should encourage multiples to develop a unique sense of self. She recounts how she and her sisters lived apart for many years beginning in their late adolescence. Now, they are all settled in long-term relationships and live close to one another in their native country of Norway. Kari remains convinced that their time apart played a significant role in normalizing their sisterly bonds and empowering each of them to form healthy attachments with significant others.

Overall, *Parent like a Triplet* is an outstanding addition to parenting literature that educates multiples and nonmultiples alike about the special developmental trajectory, needs, and challenges of same-age siblings.

Joan A. Friedman, Ph.D.

Dr Joan A. Friedman is one of the world's leading twin experts. She's an identical twin and a mother of five, including fraternal twin sons, and has specialized in the psychology of twins. This gives her truly unique insight as she can combine the personal perspective of being a twin, raising twins and insight from research and counselling twins and twin parents.

Friedman has authored three books on the psychology of twins: Emotionally Healthy Twins, The Same but Different, and Twins in Session.
www.joanafriedmanphd.com

INTRODUCTION

One became *multiple*

Like everyone else, I began life as a fertilized egg. But mine—well, mine kept on splitting. One became *multiple*.

This book is everything I have learned from being an identical triplet, everything I've ever wondered about and everything I wish my parents had read before my sisters and I came into the world. It's the book I wish someone had thrust into my hand as a teenager and that everyone around me had read. In short, it's what I hope is a funny but also secretly serious look at what it means to be a multiple, whether identical or fraternal.

This book is a parental battle guide to twins and triplets

I began thinking about writing this book when I turned 31. That's when it hit me. It could have been me: that was my mother's age when we were born. It's also the time I realized that if I were to offer any advice at all, I had to be able to speak only as someone's child and not already be a parent who, let's face it, would know better than dish out advice left, right and center to anyone juggling multiple babies.

Indeed, I drafted most of this book before I had a child of my own, which at times means an author with expectations on the other side of reasonable. But throughout it is a book written with lots of love for parents of multiples, meant to amuse, comfort, and above all make you think, *Ah-ha, I get it now.*

If you're a parent looking for practical tips on how to foster individuality in your children and the bond between them, I got you. On the small-scale, I will tell you how to dress your children so that others can make them out as different people, why shared gifts are right up there with liver stew, homework and early bedtimes, and how to make sure a shared birthday still becomes each little person's very special day. I'll also tell you what psychologists say about twins' shared social world as little, how comparisons and competitions play out, and why our quest for individuality is more driven than what most people experience.

What's also in this book are all the things you might not think about or be aware of as a parent, like why you should scrap the word 'separation' for 'pause' whenever you ponder some alone time for your children, why your children might not perceive each other as in-built best buddies, and how to avoid the frankly bleak situation where they feel responsible for their co-multiples' happiness at all times.

Many parents will undoubtedly find comfort in reading about the life-sustaining bond many multiples enjoy (indeed, we live longer than singletons—and that would be the Bridget Jones-y term researchers have come up with for all non-multiples—due to our close social bonds), but only going on about the wonderful bits won't resolve the things that make it trickier than necessary to be a multiple. This book is therefore also my beef with the many myths surrounding twins and triplets, about pitfalls to steer clear of or hiccups to anticipate.

Because I genuinely believe that if I can do my part in pointing out what's clearly and obviously not working, we can deal with that and then go back to belly laughs.

And related to that, this is a book that gives some insight into a seeming twin and triplet conundrum: If we truly enjoy the closest bond between people on this planet, why do many of us opt for some geographical distance between ourselves and our fellow clones come adult life? For much of our adult lives, my triplet sisters and I have chosen to study, work and live in different countries. I once made a triplet mother cry after telling her this, for she saw a broken bond looming on the horizon for her boys if they were to spend long periods apart. On the contrary, I told her: it might enable them to hold onto their closeness.

This book is also a triplet's quest to finding answers to all things multiple

Fellow identical twins, triplets and quads are likely to be just as baffled as I first was when I learnt that we indeed fit the very definition of a clone, that people mistake us because brains function like lazy archiving systems, pausing at whoever first fits most of the criteria, and how we really should have rooted for being either first born or first home from hospital as that multiple tends to become the parental favorite. I also hope you will enjoy hearing someone else discuss the many irks of sharing DNA, like having positively unhelpful siblings point out issues with your body because it's their body too, of people losing all common sense in their quest to find differences where they expect there to be none, and obviously, how tricky it is at times to be perceived as *potayto, potahto*.

And for all fraternal multiples, who perhaps picked up this book to learn if the grass is in any way greener, I trust you will be relieved to learn that you in many ways pulled the longest straw. Researchers say your parents were more likely to let you go your own ways when little and pushed less hard on your twin identity. You might be surprised nonetheless to learn of the 'couple's effect', of how nurture, that would be your environment, might have masked your true nature and that having some time apart from your co-multiple(s) as an adult might indeed have made you more like your twin.

That said, whether we share 100% (identicals) or 50% of our DNA (fraternals, just like regular siblings) with someone else, fraternals and identicals are fellow team members. We face comparable challenges and growing up as a multiple is psychologically more challenging than growing up a singleton, whether you're of the identical or fraternal type. More so than typical siblings, we need additional help in figuring ourselves out as unique individuals. Also, the many myths about what it mean to be a twin makes it harder for all of us: many fraternals feel cheated of the status as 'proper twins' (no doubt this happens more in in France where fraternals are tactlessly known as 'faux jumeaux', meaning false multiples) and most multiples face the challenge of being constantly compared with just the one or two.

And, if you're a partner of a twin or triplet hoping for some input that will help you understand the bond between multiples, it's in here as well. You might like to jump directly to chapter 17 where I have tucked in anecdotes and research to make you immediately look more gently at your partner and where I also prove the Internet forum user 'Twinhell' wrong: the twin bond is not marriage kryptonite.

Worldwide there are more than 125 million living multiples.[1] That is equivalent to the population of Mexico. So, who am I to tell you all of this?

Obviously, I don't hold the answers to what it's like to be a multiple. Partly because of the statistics at hand, which hold that a pair of identical twins is born every 50 seconds[2] and reveal that one in 30 pregnancies results in twins while one in 1000 ends up as triplets.[3,4]

Add to that the fact that it's not just down to whom you ask but also at what age they are when you ask them. The experience of being a multiple is not a constant, it's a scale. And in my life, I have slid up and down that scale.

If you'd met me at sixteen, when I was finally on my own— on the other side of the world as an exchange student in Costa Rica for a year—you would never have known I was a multiple. It was a chance to be just me in the world—there was simply no way anything would be about the three of us unless I told people about my sisters. So I didn't. Halfway into the year, when my triplet sister Mariann flew down from Guatemala, where she was an exchange student, for a two-week visit, people around me were startled.

"Whoa, I never knew!"

"What, there's two of you?"

No, just the one, I recall thinking.

Yet, if you'd asked me about being a triplet at the ages of eight or ten, however, I wouldn't have known what to answer. Self-reflection hadn't kicked in.

"I've never known or been anything else," I would have protested at your silly question before, depending on the day, also telling you:

a) It's so, so much fun. While Mum and Dad were out, we raided the cupboards and made *six* cakes. Two were actually edible.

b) It's rubbish. They beat me to our shared underwear drawer and only the bad pants were left.

c) They're both really stupid.

If you had asked the four-year-old me, I wouldn't have understood your question. I know that for a fact, because a family legend says we came running home from the playground one day to tell Mum and Dad the news: "Did you know that we're *triplets*?"

"Yes," they told us, "we knew that."

But, between the ages of twelve and seventeen, I was hyper-aware of the fact that I was a triplet. This was the time of my life when I was trying the hardest to figure out who I was in the world, while everyone else seemed content filing me under "the triplet." I often thought of how much easier life would have been if I'd been a singleton, a fraternal twin, or someone else, anyone else, someone who wouldn't have been mistaken for my sisters. Someone who would be *seen*. Someone who wouldn't always be *compared*.

And today? Today I believe I won life's jackpot.

Thankfully, my aim is not to speak on behalf of all multiples but to make you *feel* what it might be like to be a multiple, especially of the identical kind. Other books on twins and triplets, prime contenders being those written by parents, will contain vast more advice on the practicalities of twins and triplets than this book. That's not my ballgame. I am here to shed some light on the psychology of growing up a multiple, and to do so from a child's perspective.

In this book, you will find plenty of studies and facts, but I've carefully tucked in anecdotes as I believe you're more likely to remember the advice I seek to share if I tell stories rather than just letting you piece together statistics and academic studies.

Now, a little caveat before we properly begin: Most of the stories I'm told about my childhood starts with the words "one of you". Yet, this is entirely my story. And, just like life itself, being a multiple is a messy story, full of paradoxes we all happily live with.

So, here's ~~ours~~ mine.

CHAPTER 1

Twinning: how one can become multiple

In which I tell you how identical twins and triplets might have been one possible person for some mind-boggling 300 hours, thank philosophers for saying we have nonetheless never been anyone but ourselves, and run through the basic biology of both fraternal and identical multiples happening. I also share why I think of our time in the womb as a crowded affair, more like a mad dash for the exit rather than the so often portrayed animated slumber party.

On Sunday, 16 May 1982, at 00.15 p.m., my parents' lives changed forever. Then again at 00.17 p.m. And at 00.19 p.m. as well. Three perfectly healthy girls entered their lives.

My parents had been expecting two, as that was what the ultrasound images had shown and that's what the doctors had told them. But that's not what happened. As soon as my mother sat back in relief, after the birth of Mariann and I, hushed conversations commenced among the hospital staff.

"Why are you whispering?" my mother had demanded to know of the doctor and staff as they crowded around her.

"We think there may be another one in there," came the reply.

Then, as if that weren't enough, there was the revelation of the potential fourth daughter. The day after my mother had given birth, the doctors said they had found another embryo, the size of a thumb, still attached to the placenta and would my parents by any chance like to see it? They politely declined.

This was back in the eighties, well before in vitro fertilization (IVF) multiplied (pun intended) the frequency of twins and triplets in this world. Clearly, it was also way before ultrasound technology could say with certainty how many fetuses you were carrying. As a child, the story of how only two at a time appeared during ultrasounds made me imagine our time in the womb as a months-long game of hide and seek: Who had gone into hiding? Who had popped into sight? Whose existence was unknown?

Anyways, such was the sensation that three nurses remained outside the delivery room entrance, waiting for my father to arrive so they could share the pleasure of telling him the news. My father didn't make the labor in time, as he had to arrange child care for our two brothers, twenty-month-old Stig and eight-year-old Tord. (Yes, that made ours a family household of four children in diapers.)

My parents said no when local, regional, and national newspapers and magazines started calling the following day, but eventually the doctors pleaded with them to reconsider. This was a great achievement for them, that we were all delivered safely, and would my parents by any chance be okay with at least granting the local newspaper an interview?

Fortunately for the doctors, my parents said yes. The article also landed my parents one-year's supply of diapers for their triplets, courtesy of a diaper company. (To imagine the quantities involved with diapering triplets for an entire year—at about twenty diaper changes for every one of those 365 days—picture a ten-square-meter room stacked from floor to ceiling and door to wall with diapers. Then picture my father, when those ran out, divvying up diaper purchases because he found it so embarrassing to buy the necessary quantity from just one shop.)

As an adult, I can't get past the fact that my mother delivered all of us in less than four minutes. As a child, however, much of this had me tangled up in thoughts. What were the chances of *me* happening?

My parents met on Stord, a small island off the southwest coast of Norway with just over 11,000 inhabitants at the time and a ferry connection to the mainland. My father moved there from Stavanger, Norway's fourth-largest city, to become a teacher and soon the star of the island's football team. My mother dreamed of becoming an architect, but that would mean leaving the island for a larger city, a cost her family couldn't bear, or so my grandfather told her, saying she should first aim for the education available on the island, which meant teachers' college. Indeed, she opted to become a kindergarten teacher and met my father at a local dance.

I was always fascinated by this story. *They met—I happened. They hadn't met—I wouldn't have happened.* But, the chances of *me* were much, much slimmer: not only did they have to meet, but the specific, fertilized egg they eventually produced had to split into four, and I needed to be one of the three parts that made it into a little human being.

How does twinning occur?

Fraternal multiples

When people speak of multiples "running in the family," they're referring to fraternal multiples, not identical ones. Genetically, fraternal twins are like other siblings; one sperm and one egg for each twin, and the fused egg and sperm (now a zygote) ends up as just one person.[5] Fraternal twins come about when additional eggs are released during ovulation. The norm is to release just one, but some women release several eggs at a time, due to a complex mix of events including a genetic trait in the mother's family, maternal height and weight, and number of previous pregnancies (which means that a question of "should we have one more?" is sometimes answered with two!).[6] As a rule of thumb, fraternal twins have their own placenta, but these may sometimes overlap or fuse.[7]

Identical multiples

Identical multiples are life at its most random. A fertilized egg is not supposed to split. Why it does remain a mystery to researchers.[8] It's assumed to be a malfunction[9] or, "the world's most beautiful handicap," as one doctor put it to my parents.

Up until two weeks after conception, the zygote can divide in two, resulting in twins, or split further[10], resulting in even "higher order multiples," which is the rather bland term some researchers use for triplets, quadruplets, and quintuplets. Other experts fortunately use what is among my favorite scientific designations: "super twins,"[11] admittedly, a term I want to try next time I'm out and about with one of my sisters and we're asked if we're twins.

"No, we're *super* twins!"

The most common situation for identical twins is a split four to eight days after conception. If the zygote splits before then, each twin will have a separate placenta. If it happens later, the chances of complications increase. Siamese twins, in which the fertilized egg splits only partially, occur if the splitting starts after twelve days.[12]

The basic setup for most identical triplets is that the fertilized egg splits, and then one of the resultant cells splits again. There is also another way: a four-way split. In this case, identical triplets start out as identical quadruplets. After a first split of the zygote (identical twins), both cells split again. And, as in our case, the potential quadruplets become triplets when only three embryos grow to maturity.[13]

What are the odds of this happening? Slim, even for multiples themselves when they are looking to conceive (or as my husband once joked, "You know I'm only with you because you said identical multiples are random and not hereditary, right?") My sisters and I were spontaneously conceived (so no IVF or other type of medical help that increases the chances of having multiples), and there hadn't been any twins or triplets in either my parents' families prior to us either.

When does identical twinning occur?

A part of me really likes the idea that my sisters and I started out in an unrehearsed yet synchronized swim toward the uterus as one zygote. Perhaps because we've been growing in tandem ever since, clocking in those milk teeth, centimeters, and first grey hairs at the same time, it seems only fitting that we developed together as that first ball of cells as well.

But what's difficult for me to accept is how long I was truly "one" with my sisters as the same zygote before it split. It probably took you some ten seconds to read that last paragraph, which was my earlier notion of how long the entire ordeal took. The few seconds it took before nature tossed a coin, got heads up, and exclaimed exuberantly, "Oh yes, I'm going to make *many* of this kind and there shall be *lots* of possible futures for this zygote!"

I've always pictured the split as I imagine a bacterial colony explosion in a Petri dish. It turns out, however, that it's not a matter of seconds or even milliseconds in which our existence as identical multiples is determined: my sisters and I were possibly one for up to two weeks before it was decided that we would be several possible persons instead of just the one.

Just to give you a sense of how long we're talking, my friend Google says you can do the following in 14 days' or what amounts to more than 300 hours' worth of time:

- Become a trained yoga teacher
- Complete the longest community service sentence given in the UK
- A backpacking trip by train from Amsterdam to Milan

Fortunately, the timing of the split also has people other than me tangled up in thoughts. I say fortunately because such ruinations have yielded a very elegant argument among some philosophers that helps reassure identical multiples we have never been anyone but ourselves: If you believe that humans have a soul, when does the individual start—if we can also start out as someone else, or more accurately, a combined self? Given the existence of twins, personhood can't start at conception, because if we have a soul during the period when a zygote may still split, wouldn't that leave twins with half a soul? Thankfully, that is indeed a rhetorical question, as the conclusion became that any notion of me-ness must begin at the earliest fourteen days later, when identical twinning is no longer possible.[14]

Shared DNA or not, we all emerge from the womb unique

Yet, when it comes to my me-ness, my *raison d'etre*, I prefer certainty. Thanks to researchers in the emerging field of epigenetics, even those of us who have the same DNA and crowd together in one placenta within the womb can be certain that we get born into this world as unique individuals. (Since this is chapter one and I don't want to scare you away, I've saved the deep-dive into epigenetics and all things clones for a later chapter. Read on though, as I promise I'm explaining it all with the help of Matryoshka dolls and chocolate cakes.)

Prenatal life is not an equally shared environment for any of us: environmental factors already affect us during pregnancy. For starters, the amniotic fluid is rarely distributed equally, and umbilical cords don't carry identical blood supplies. Weight differences between fraternal multiples can be explained by their different sets of genes, yet weight differences between identical multiples are the most obvious result of unequal conditions in the womb.[15]

My triplet sister Trude learned that the hard way. As she puts it, "You said I ate her!"

When we were children, we were told by our parents that there hadn't been enough food for all four embryos to fully develop, which was why three and not four were born. When we were old enough to understand our birth weights, the question of the hour obviously became: Who was the greedy one?

"I have this memory," Trude says, "of the two of you reading out loud the numbers on these embroideries hanging in the living room, the ones with cross-stitched storks and details about our birth. Nineteenhundred grams, twothousandtwo-hundred grams, twothousandtwohundred*andforty*! You kept asking me why I had to eat so much. You were both smaller than me, so obviously I could have gotten by on less food."

Perhaps thanks to this story, I wasn't that surprised when I read the findings of Italian researcher Alessandra Piontelli, trained in medicine and neuropsychiatry. She observed the behavior of thirty pairs of twins in the womb, and was the first to debunk fantasies of twins cuddling each other in the womb. While some twins appeared to avoid contact, others showed an inclination towards touch or closeness of some kind. Yet, she warns, we shouldn't read much into this. While the fetuses may feel the touch of the other, that's a far cry from interpreting that sensation and giving it meaning.[16] In other words, there's a big difference between *'something just touched me'* versus *'I got a cuddle!'*

Cuddle or not, Piontelli's warning is nonetheless one to take to heart. As we'll see throughout this book, our culture's idealized notion of twins, so the perception of twins as lifelong soulmates, often translates into misconceptions and myths that make it harder than necessary to go about this life as a multiple – and an individual.

CHAPTER 2

Why 'how do you do it?" is the world's most grating question for parents of multiples

There is one question parents of multiples will face more often than, "Are they *all* yours?" and that is, "How do you do it?". Yet why does the standard reply of "you find a way" prompt sympathetic smiles, "it-must-be-horrible" faces, and apparent disbelief? It is, let's be honest, because the rest of us dig for perceived misery. Yet, to all you parents who are *nailing* multiple babies, I ask you to look gently on us. Know that one day your own children will ask the same question— in utter awe. Until then, let us look at how to best answer intrusive strangers and thoughtless neighbors.

When we were to be brought home from hospital, our brother Stig, just under two years old at the time, came along. His first comment when he saw us? "Are we going to take *all* the hospital's babies?"

Surprise at the sheer number of simultaneous babies is not necessarily handled with more sophistication by adults. I once listened to a radio show where triplet parents spoke of the need to build in what they called "gawp time" whenever they went out, meaning time spent waiting while strangers peeked into the pram, asked questions, or just marveled at the little ones.

It's like a public relations job, one said, referring to all the questions from strangers. "If you are a private person, keen to keep to yourself, don't have triplets," was the brilliant advice of another.

Parents of multiples refuse the assumption tucked underneath the question

As all parents eventually realize, life with multiples is indeed like Nike's slogan, pushing your limits to *Just Do It.* You knuckle through the first weeks or months of sleeplessness, exhaustion, and bewilderment, and then, as with anything, do something often enough and you figure it out. Or, as my father puts it, "routines, routines, routines."

Poll whomever you want—I'm pretty certain that the simple act of parading around multiple babies who look happy, healthy, and clean-ish will make anyone think of parents of multiples as magical unicorns, and most will inevitably ask these parents how they're coping.

Thus, I was surprised when I first learned from the Internet that parents of multiples dislike the question of how they're coping. It's right up there with:

- "Are they all natural?" ("No, this one is an alien")
- "Were they IVF?" ("No, missionary. How's your sex life?")
- And: "Are they identical?" ("Almost; the boy is a bit different from the girls.")

As my father said, "I sometimes felt that people were digging for misery, that when they asked, they expected things to be horrible. And it's a bit like when people ask if you're in a bad mood—you *are* in a bad mood after that. So yes, at times it was hard, but it was also incredibly nice. You were so cute, and it was a beautiful sight: three freshly washed babies on the floor in their PJs, playing and pushing each other around a bit."

In an article aptly called *Triple Delight*, British comedian and mother of four (triplets and a singleton), Jackie Clune tells the same tale. She believes people asking about her children crave stories of (perceived) misfortune, of how she feels dreadful, exhausted, and depressed. "No one wants to hear that we are having a lovely time with our babies, who have started to smile all at once this week and are sleeping in blissful four-hour chunks all of a sudden, and are so bright-eyed and lively after their bath that we feel like cracking open a bottle of champagne just to give them the party they seem to be up for."[17]

What's the takeaway here, beyond that apparently post-bath time is triplet parent bliss? The answer is in our local libraries.

Question of a seesaw: the reason parents of multiples present the glossy version

Parents land book deals for part-memoirs, part-survival guides with titles like *The Shock of Becoming a Mother*,[18] *After Labor—What Everyone Forgot to Say*,[19] and (yes, this is a real book title) *Let Mummy Poop in Peace*.[20] As one of these authors put it, someone had to put pen to paper and tell the truth about how tough it can be to have a baby.[21] *One baby*. So, when parents of multiples say two or three's a breeze, the world, infinitely skeptical, replies, "Really?"

I sometimes wonder how many times parents of multiples have had someone tell them, *I can barely manage with one, so how are you coping with three?* And there it is, the assumption that's often tucked beneath the question of how you're coping: you're not. Not *really* coping. You can't be.

But you are.

But, just like most parents, you will at one point battle guilt over not being the parent you would have wanted to be. And if you're indeed a parent of multiples reading this, I'm willing to bet that you are in for some particularly hard rounds of self-bashing. Just like any parent, my father and triplet mother Clune had the stories to satisfy the quest for misery. So why did neither of them want to share? My theory is that it comes down to the seesaw principle. Let me explain.

Brief conversations don't allow for nuance and detailed explanation, so if someone asks how you are doing but pushes hard on the negatives, you cling to the positives to get the balance right, just like on a seesaw.

There you are, happily queuing at the supermarket, enjoying a little break from the circus troupe at home, when a neighbor engages you in what they perceive as friendly small-talk. *You sure have your hands full, huh? I can't imagine how you do it. I struggle with one!*

I get it: a seemingly sympathetic face when you're brimming with pride and feel like you earned a high-five and a note of congratulations more than anything else. It's like having scored a winning goal and waiting for spectators to join together in applause, but none comes and instead you get a meek "Hang in there!" over the speakers. *Now, wait a minute,* you find yourself protesting, *Didn't you just see what I did? I scored! I just washed and fed three little girls, last week I dealt with a triple onset of chickenpox, and yesterday they all slept through the night.* Then you push harder than you otherwise would have on the positives; you can't let anyone in on all the missed passes and free kicks at twenty yards, the ones that hit the goalpost. You need to make sure the winning goal becomes part of the match sum-up.

Five suggested ways to answer, *'How in the world are you coping?!'*

As a parent of multiples, you might find it easier to deal with this and other twin- or triplet-related questions if you remember that you're on the easy end of multiples quizzing. Sooner or later your children will be the ones answering the questions from strangers, neighbors, and relatives. You are the pseudo-celebrity for a few years, but your kids are in it for the long haul. One day you will need to sit them down to explain that it's normal for people to ask questions or want to look at someone that's "unusual," or at least out of the norm. That is a conversation that is a lot easier to have if your children have seen you politely answer or fend off similar questions over the years.

To help you out, here are therefore some ways to answer and think about this:

1. ~~Tell the truth~~

Not really an option. This is a long story, and you have multiples to look after.

2. Lie through your teeth

If you ever feel like biting a person's head off, remember the best way to annoy someone is to remain cheerful. Tell your most adorable twin or triplet story, like how one's laughter sets off the others, how they have discovered each other as playmates. Or bring out the big guns and speak of how they sleep through the night (even if they don't).

There is nothing that brings out the hate more in fellow sleep-deprived parents than stories of a baby who sleeps through the night. *Multiple* babies sleeping blissfully should do the trick.

3. Bring out the laughs.

Say it's a matter of the Stockholm syndrome: you've fallen in love with your captors. Then wink at your children if they're next to you.

4. Realize it's small-talk—and remember that most people who ask are in awe.

In terms of small-talk, bonding over how tiring parenting is might seem preferable to talking about the weather. Most are also utterly unaware that they're the fifth person just that week to ask you how you cope. Deep down you know that, but you've been up half the night and have no intention of letting people in on it. Because you *are* coping. You're nailing multiples!

Still, don't let this opportunity pass you by. When people empathetically ask how you're coping, that's your cue to reply, "Our sanity saver is when people help out. You free to babysit any time soon?"

5. Take their word for it. This is on *them*, not you.

Tackling people who dish out unhelpful comments like "Better you than me!" or "I would kill myself if that happened to me" is much easier if you take them at their word. Chances are, if someone keeps pushing, trying their best to get you to admit to domestic havoc, they're struggling themselves. If you say raising twins or even triplets is a piece of cake, where does that leave the rest of us? After all, how do you complain about having one when the one with two or three babies is around? It's simple: you don't.

What my siblings and I know well: "You know we can never complain to Dad, right?"

As long as I can remember, whenever my siblings and I have spoken about having children, we've quickly added that no matter how long, long, long a particular night with a baby might have seemed, there would be no way we could let our father in on it.

Our father laughs whenever we say these things. "I've told you the story about the teacher's lounge, right?" he says. "If one of the other parents were complaining about how they were sleep deprived or exhausted and they didn't see me at first, well, as soon as they saw me—the one with three babies at home—they'd go all quiet."

The first time my sister Mariann and I brought our children—*one* each—to our father's, we were bonding over being tired. Then we heard a chuckle behind us. "What about me? I had five!" our father said. Mariann and I exchanged a quick look and changed the topic.

Yes, you can play your triplet trump card, or you can make it possible for others to also vent a bit.

When my son was six weeks old and my father was visiting, I told him for the first time just how totally exhausted I was. All I could think of was how each day lasted a million hours and how sleep felt like a distant memory. Dad and I headed out for take-away coffees, but as soon as we came outside I put a hand on his shoulder. I needed a hug. The kind of hug you don't want to let go of. (Well, at least I didn't. My father eventually did.) I started to cry. "I can't do this," I said. "*How* did you do it?"

He smiled. "Let's go for a walk."

Coffees in hand, I shared the kind of story so many new parents tell, part of me hoping for magical advice, part of me just wanting him to know that I was in awe. Because they *did* do it. "How did you do it?" was as much a statement as a question as far as I was concerned.

That's when my father threw me a lifeline. "Remember, it might be just as tough to have one child if, for example, if that child just screams and screams."

Mine wasn't a screamer, but my father was giving me much-needed permission to be exhausted. It was just what I needed, even if I had just the one.

So, if you're a parent of multiples, the next time the question of "how you cope" comes along, you should pat yourself on the back and know that one day your own children will ask you the very same question in absolute, utter awe. *How did you do it?* Because you did. You coped. *You did it!*

CHAPTER 3

Need a pep talk before having multiples? Here you go!

Parenting multiples hits most people like a ton of, well, diapers. When you're overwhelmed, when you think you can't possibly cope, it's not because you're failing: it's because you're *human*. At this very moment, there are thousands of people in need of a pep-talk, thousands of people who think parenting multiples is bigger and more than they ever expected. This piece is the pep-talk I wish someone had given my mother during her postnatal depression, what I want everyone who expects multiples to know and everyone around them as well.

"I think we *made the decision* to cope, and that has seen us through the tough times."[22]

That's what triplet parent and British comedian Jackie Clune says in her book *Extreme Motherhood*, which details her pregnancy and first year with triplets.

"Stubborn with lots of optimism."[23]

That's my Mum's explanation when asked how she managed to do it all.

It's from an interview in a women's magazine from when the Norwegian prime minister invited my mother to her office for a one-on-one coffee and a chat. Well, almost just the two of them, a journalist and photographer came along to cover the event of Gro Harlem Brundtland handing my mother a red, potted Christmas flower. (More about that later).

Both quotes are two triplet mothers' spin on our society's generic pep talk of, "You can do anything if you set your mind to it." At first glance, a motto to take to heart; people do discover unknown strength when the going gets tough. Also, a week as a triplet parent averaging 200 diaper changes, 200 feedings, and 60 tiny fingernails and toenails to trim probably seems a whole lot easier with a positive spin on life.

The generic pep-talk of 'achieving anything you set your mind to' is problematic

At its heart is Isaac Newton's third law of motion, *For every action, there is an equal and opposite reaction.* Action: reaction. Think boundlessly positive: scale that mountain. But if it's seemingly all on you, then it's also on you if you come up short, making it scarily easy to let feelings of inadequacy, guilt, and shame overwhelm you. Because what happens if you were determined to cope, that you assumed you would, because you normally have a pretty good handle on life, and then you find that you can't?

You might have expected to go down the route of triplet parent Jackie Clune, who one year into triplet motherhood sums up her experience with, "It has been very hard at times, but in general I am amazed to say that Dad was right—having these babies have been the best thing that has ever happened to me." A truly extraordinary event, she says, and as if preempting raised eyebrows, quickly adding: "I know how cheesy, rose-tinted and irritating this probably sounds, but I don't care because it's the truth, and it feels necessary to acknowledge the good things about having three at once in face of so much perceived misfortune."[24]

But, then you end up on the same path as my mother, "She just cried and cried," my father says of her postnatal depression "She cried a lot, said she couldn't do this. 'I can't do this, Per Ivar.'"

The first time I heard about my parents' rocky start with triplet parenthood, I was in my late twenties, at home at my father's for a visit at the same time as my sisters. In the middle of the fairly casual conversation, one of my sisters turned to our father and asked, "How in the world did you manage when we were babies?"

Now, these are his standard replies:

- The cheerful: "I've suppressed your first years—*ha ha ha.*"
- The stoic: "You find a way. I've always believed that people are adaptable."
- The straightforward: "Well, what was the alternative?"

But this time was different. He went for this one: "It was tough. Mum got postnatal depression after having you. At one point, she suggested giving one of you away."

My sisters and I didn't dare to move. We just kept our coffee cups still in our hands and stared straight at our father, probably all thinking that if we just kept quiet, he might go on. He had sat on this for more than twenty years.

PARENT LIKE A TRIPLET

But the pause dragged on, so in the end one of us asked, "*Erm... give one of us away?*"

"Yes. To Anna and Marthon."

Mum had said it didn't seem fair. Their closest friends who lived just down the road struggled to conceive and then she and Dad were the ones ending up with triplets after already having had two boys. "So, there was a period that autumn I was really concerned," my father said. "Not about taking care of you. That was based a bit on the principle of an assembly line."

(This, more or less, is what it looked like as well. One of my husband's favorites among my childhood photos shows us three babies in high chairs with my mother in front, holding a bowl of porridge and one spoon. If you failed to open when the spoon came around, it simply bounced on to the next.)

Back to Dad. "I was really concerned about Mum, how that would go. We didn't really have a network around us, and our family lived far away. In the beginning, the municipality provided us with a person who would come around and help, but after a short period, we were told that we were two resourceful people and would need to manage on our own. Well, resourceful or not, we replied, we still need to sleep," he said.

He paused. My father is fine with pauses. He likes to say that his boys are more like him, and his girls more like their mother, "much more verbal". I think he could add impatient to that.

But, again, the pause dragged on. He needed a little nudge. "So... give one of us away. What did you say?"

"I said no."

"Thank you!" my sisters and I chorused, making all of us laugh.

"You know I asked her about it a few months later. *'Noooo,'* she said. Refused. Said she had never said it."

More laughter. It was easy to imagine our mother shaking her head in disbelief once the depression had lifted.

"Deep down, she probably didn't mean it," my father said, "but there and then she felt like she wasn't enough. It was something she said in desperation. Wouldn't it be better for the children to be with someone else, someone who could offer what she felt she couldn't?"

Depression is alarmingly common among parents of multiples

While I was surprised to learn of my mother's depression, what hit me hard was the fact that she never told us herself. Mum passed away when we were fifteen from epilepsy, and I get that the moment might never have felt right to tell teenagers that their existence brought on depression. Perhaps it was a time she didn't feel like revisiting; perhaps it was no joke that she'd suppressed parts of it. But it might also be because we don't talk about depression as we should. If we did, we'd realize how common it is, and the ones at the bottom of a well they feel unable to climb out of would realize that they're not there alone.

Of all new mothers, even those having one baby at a time, one in every ten battles postnatal depression.[25] For mothers of multiples, studies put the figure in the range of seventeen[26] to twenty-five percent,[27] so suffice to say it's alarmingly common. As a parent of twins and triplets, there's no doubt more guilt and exhaustion, more to take on, and more to make you feel like you're failing to cope.[28]

In a study by Twins Trust of 1,300 mothers of twins and 70 of triplets in the UK, mothers spoke of feeling ashamed or guilty they might be facing a postnatal depression, because they were supposed to be coping. As one said, "It is hard to be honest because you feel you will be judged a 'bad mother.'" More than half had thoughts of wanting to walk away from their babies. Nine percent felt this desire "frequently." Mothers who had already had children said they found it difficult to balance the new babies with the needs of their existing children. Close to half said they spent less than an hour a day talking to another adult.

A researcher who followed seventeen Swedish triplet families for nine years reports that the feeling of loneliness and isolation is much stronger for triplet mothers than for twin mothers.[29] Speaking of the constant round-the-clock care that triplet parents give, she also points to the obvious practicalities: "To carry twins, one on each arm, is difficult, but to carry triplets around is impossible for the mother."[30]

As a child I remember holding my father's hand as we walked up the road toward our house. Or holding two fingers. One of my sisters held the other three as we tried not to stumble over each other's feet. My two-years older brother and my other sister held onto his other hand. Reminiscing over those days, my father once told me, "Going to the shop just with two of you felt like a luxury. Then I had a hand for each!"

Here is the improved pep-talk for all parents of multiples

This pep-talk finds place in Tibet—a place that will help elucidate some key points, including that life's about making choices.

For starters, if you're intent on scaling a mountain like Mount Everest, it's obvious that positive thinking alone won't get you to the top: a whole lot of Sherpas will. You're also going to make damn sure you take breaks at regular intervals to regain your strength, and if the going gets too tough, you'll hurry down to lower altitudes where you'll proudly pat yourself on the back for catching those signs in time, all so you still stand a chance at going back at it. You are obviously going to the top, but nobody, not even yourself, expects you to go straight-up in one go all on your own.

Let's get started, shall we?

1. It _is_ a big deal: _do not_ diminish your role.

In regular pep-talks, we tend to downplay and compare, like when I asked my father what he would have told himself if he had met himself on the way in to see his triplet daughters for the first time.

"I would have told him, this will go well. People have had much larger challenges in life than this. Take one day at a time, I would have said."

I'm all in favor of reminders that others face larger obstacles and there's comfort in knowing that others have coped beautifully with what you're about to embark on. But there's no need to diminish your role either.

Again, think climbing in Tibet. _No one_ climbs Everest and goes, "Ah, it's really no big deal. Yes, it's the highest mountain in the world, but it's *not* considered the world's most difficult to climb. Thousands have already made it to the top and there's even a few hundred other climbers on this mountain right now. So *blah blah blah*, no biggie."

No one in their right mind says that, so why should you?

"Would you say it's okay to say it's tremendously tough?" I asked my father.

"Well, yes," he replied before the stoic in him again got the upper hand. "And that's how it is with people. We have opportunities to get our act together when we have to. What would we do if we weren't able to take care of you three? There's a small pride in being able to say, *'I'm going to do this!'* in the back of your head.'

"When we saw that you grew and thrived and were healthy… that was itself a small victory. We spoke with pride about how we would do it. Mum was at her proudest when she could dress you up and show you off. Now parents show the children to the world on Facebook with photos and so forth on birthdays. The parallel to our time was that Mum could take you out in the pram and show you off to neighbors and friends in the village. That was Facebook in our days. To show that we managed."

They managed. They scaled that mountain. Three children, warm and fed, out on a walk with an incredibly loving parent. One thousand parental points earned.

2. Focus on "must haves," not "nice to haves".

Staying sane as a parent of multiples also comes down to what my father says when we talk of parenting, "Of course, we didn't do what you do."

Like most other parents nowadays, I'm either down on my knees playing with my son or I'm busy googling the shit out of *how to encourage independent play* to counter the hovering over him that's led us to this situation. Also, no child out there *needs* "Bach to Baby," "Sing & Sign," or any other of the myriad baby classes on offer. But their mother might.

"It helped keep *me* sane," a friend said of her decision to enroll in a baby class *every* day while on parental leave. She needed to get out and socialize, so she did. Her child didn't. In fact, he slept blissfully through most of these classes.

Therefore, here's a new motto to embrace wholeheartedly: "Everything you manage to do is a bonus!" It belongs to a friend who is one of the most positive people I know. I'm confident that part of her happiness stems from being gloriously generous with metaphorical golden stars, both to herself and others.

So, you couldn't make it out on a walk today? Well, so what! You fed them, changed them and you hugged them. A day well done! Because once you've covered those three basics of parenting infants, the rest is a bonus. Not "must haves," but a whole lot of "nice to haves." You might of course be able to pull it off, but what's the point of juggling at 8,848 meters above sea level?

3. Only crazy people go at it alone: let go of control and accept help.

People who climb Mount Everest bring Sherpas, even the ones who call themselves "solo" climbers. Because sometimes the smartest thing to do, if you are to succeed, is to ask for and accept help. It's even possible for more than a dozen people to stand together on the summit top. Yet, as surprising as this sounds to everyone else, parents of multiples sometimes dread asking for help, whether out of pride or a feeling that they really should cope on their own.

Thankfully, experts are around to tell you to lower your expectations to yourself and accept that you won't be able to meet your babies' every need on your own.[31] In the short-term, you might be able to pull it off. But in the long-term, putting that oxygen mask on yourself as well makes all the sense in the world. After all, parents are at their best when they're not collapsing of fatigue and depression.

Every third weekend as of nine months of age, my sisters and I would spend a weekend with friends of my parents. Our two-year older brother camped at a second family's, and our oldest brother stayed at home for two baby-free days with our parents.

I am tremendously happy that my parents somehow managed to find slivers of downtime, either because one took over for an hour while the other rested or because they had amazing people around who took in multiple (ha!) babies at a time. I'm equally happy that when my siblings and I came back from being away, we were all smiles and cheers, giving them the reassurance that this was a golden set-up for absolutely everyone.

I cherish the memories of those weekends, so I was puzzled when I first read a comment on a triplet forum by a parent wondering if she could bring in other people to help take care of her trio or whether that would negatively affect her bond with her children. In the forum, several parents offered reassurance, saying her triplets have each other.

They're right. It's perhaps what surprised me most while working on this book. Researchers point to the bond between twins and triplets and label it a primary attachment.[32,33] It's a term that refers to the person with whom a child develops the strongest emotional bond, usually the mother. Yet, multiples not only have a vertical pattern of attachment, so with a parent, but also a strong horizontal bond, so with each other. Italian researcher Alessandra Piontelli, who studied thirty sets of twins from pregnancy to early childhood years, explains how the attachment between the twins formed with "an uncommon intensity and at an unusually early age", noting that this was particularly solid and secure in the case of identical twins.[34] Piontelli explains: "The most constant and steady presence in the life of any twin is its co-twin. In many cases, sooner or later, each necessarily became the major figure of attachment of the other. Twins began to rely on each other for comfort, company and support."[35]

See, your children will be fine also without you now and then.

4. Do something for you.

Why do people climb Mount Everest? The most famous reply is "because it's there," but they're of course all doing it for themselves. When I was a new parent, I turned to my father—a novice parent asking a veteran—and asked him if he had any advice.

He thought for a few seconds, and then said something unexpected. I assumed he'd focus on my son, but he focused on *me*.

"Make sure that you stay you, that you don't lose yourself. You have always had opinions and kept up with politics and current affairs; do that still. I think that's important for your own sanity. Make sure you also have your own life."

Both my parents kept a small drawer open in their lives to places where they could be more than Mum and Dad. In addition to their jobs, they pursued their own interests. Ever since the age of six, my father has loved football. At the time of writing, he's just turned 70 and prides himself on every 'nutmeg' he does during the regular Monday soccer practices for the 'Old Boys' team he plays for, which consist of just as many twenty- and thirty-year-olds eager to play as old foot-ballers.

"Playing football, I had a good space to breathe, so I got to use thoughts and feelings in a different way" he says.

For my mother, it was visiting Anna (the friend who almost ended up with one of us triplets), doing arts and crafts, and being active in politics, first at the municipal level then at the county level.

"This is my hobby," she'd say, ordering us out to play while she sifted through stacks of documents while probably enjoy-ing the quiet and a coffee. Six times a year she travelled to Stavanger, a larger city two hours away, and was Bente the politician, representing the Labor party in the county council. And that's my segue to the magazine article I mentioned at the beginning of this chapter.

Six years after we were born, my mother had coffee in an office in Oslo. Next to her on the sofa was Gro Harlem Brundtland, Norway's first female prime minister. Gro, as she's simply known in Norway, passes the Danish, as the journalist who covered the meeting noted in his article. That year several celebrities were asked to give a flower to someone they believed deserved the recognition. Most chose other celebrities. Gro chose an unknown local representative.

You Deserved This, Bente! ran the headline across the front cover. In a two-page spread inside, the journalist explains how my mother's a driving force in the local community, how she managed four public kindergartens, started a private kindergarten for children up until the age of seven with a private mortgage when she saw that the coverage wasn't enough, and was active in politics for the Labor party.[36]

My mother stresses in the article that she wasn't alone in accomplishing things.

"And do mention that the honor isn't mine alone. I've had good support from many people to help in everything. Especially my husband, who's a teacher in the neighboring municipality. Just think of the year I commuted weekly to the teacher's college and he had the responsibility for five children at home. To be honest I'm not so sure I would have said yes if he had wanted to do the same!" stresses Bente with a good laugh.[37]

Let's pause a bit on her last comment in case any parent reading this is still worried about the impact on the bond with their children if they allow themselves some downtime. Monday to Thursday or Friday for an entire year, my mother wasn't around; she was a weekly commuter to complete teacher's college, staying then at her parent's place on Stord.

My father says, "You were quite big then [we were age three!], and it was much easier than when you were babies. So even if it was busy, we managed to get into good routines. It wasn't anything I would call a stressful period." Let's just briefly recap that: The man managed three three-year-olds, one five-year-old and one eleven-year-old alongside a full-time job.

But what do I and my sisters remember from this period?

Wonky ponytails—for an entire year: slightly to the side, never quite in the middle like the ones Mum made. And never an option of anything but a ponytail.

Our father, not one to blow his trumpet, never mentioned having us all to himself for days on end for a full year and I only found out about the one-year commute when I read the magazine article as an adult. I wasn't the only one who was surprised. Here's what my sisters said when I told them (mind you, not in the same conversation):

Trude: "Oh my god, the man is magical. Dad did that? Give that man a medal! But—" and then she laughed "—I only remember the pony tails!"

Mariann: "*Aaaaahhhh*! A year. That's probably why we remember the pony tails?"

As they say, no good deed goes unpunished.

So, to sum-up: Give yourself an immense pat on the back before you reach out, get help and go off as well, climbing with multiples in Tibet.

As the journalist notes in the article, my mother was a person the prime minister wanted to honor as a thank you for showing others that it pays off to work hard and find new ways. She did indeed. And even she, the strongest, most stubborn and most optimistic woman I have ever known, at times found the mountain too fierce.

Clearly, there is lots of good motivation in stubbornness and positive thinking, but you also need to allow yourself to be a mere human like the rest of us. If it takes a village to raise a child, surely you can reach out and get some help if you've been dealt two or three at the same time?

And, my Mum? I asked Dad once whether he thought she would have enjoyed this kind of book when she pondered the prospect of twins, and then realized she was in for triplets. "She would have devoured it; read it in one go!," he replied. I like the thought of that, as well as Mum's saying on how people who pass away aren't really gone if someone's still thinking and speaking about them. Or writing.

.

CHAPTER 4

The big baby mix-up: parents should give themselves time to bond with their multiples

Newfound parents of multiples worry they can't tell their babies apart and multiples horror as children to learn that our parents mixed up our names. Yet, the daunting challenge lies not in keeping tabs on names, but in resisting the temptation to assign personality traits too early and finding differences where there are none. In this piece I also tell you why, as an identical, you should root hard for being the first-born or the first to leave hospital. Chances are it will land you a prime position as the parental favorite (at least in Australia).

So here I am, seven years old, and I'm not sure I'm me.

My sisters aren't entirely sure they're themselves either.

We've heard of Triplet A, Triplet B, and Triplet C, the three newborns the media was eager to cover. We know they put name tags on these babies at birth, but we're not entirely sure the name tags never fell off. We need to know to be sure.

So, we ask our parents, "Tell us, honestly, could you have mixed us up?"

"Yes," Mum says.

We stare at her, confused, and belt out a collective, "Yes!?"

"Most likely the name tags fell off at some point."

Our horror at her unguarded slip of honesty clearly register on our faces, as my father is quick to intervene, shaking his head slowly. "In the end, I don't think we mixed you up," he said, but it is a weak effort.

I spend the next few days thinking, *I could be Mariann. Could I be Trude? Or am I me?*

If you're a multiple reading this, you might not be whom you think you are

There's a scene in *Alice's Adventures in Wonderland* where Alice wakes up and has grown overnight. "Who in the world am I?" she asks herself. "Ah, that's the great puzzle!" she answers herself.[38]

Many would agree with Alice, but very few must think about what Alice considers next.

"And she began thinking over all the children she knew that were of the same age as herself, to see if she could have been changed for any of them."[39]

Sometimes I'm not sure if I'm really Kari—at least not the original one.

There are numerous Facebook groups devoted to triplets. On one of them I recently saw a great thread called, "You might be the parents of triplets if…" Among the contributions are:

- You've ever said to the in-laws helping you change diapers, "Take this guy and put him over there next to what's-his-name."

- You've ever had a child come into your room at night for comfort after a bad dream. You hug. The child goes back to bed. Your partner asks, "Who was that?" You say, "I have no idea."
- You get halfway to a hospital appointment and realize you have the wrong child!

Not surprisingly, being able to tell multiples apart seems a common concern. On a forum for parents of identical triplets, parents had this to say:

- My girls are four months old and I think I can tell them apart now. I definitely know one and the other two I can tell if they are side by side.
- My trio is four years old and my father-in-law can't tell them apart. He lives with us. I think it took until they were close to a year for us.
- One of my kids just sat on the couch. Husband: "Which one are you?" They are 8 years old.

The personalities of identical multiples often blend—and that is fine

My parents had to get to know multiple children at once—three new babies alongside a two-year-old and an eight-year-old, each developing and coloring in the bits of who they are. I truly wonder how they kept tabs on all of us (especially as I assume we were then, as now, so similar). As twin researcher Nancy Segal notes, "Parents, close friends and twins themselves tune into the differences, but anyone meeting identical twins for the first time cannot deny that their personalities often blend."[40]

My sisters and I did a personality test online once, and we all ended up with ENFP (Extrovert, Intuitive, Feeling, Perceiving). This shouldn't come as a surprise either, as a substantial portion of our personalities, twin studies say, are driven by DNA (some put the figure at twenty percent; others hike it up to fifty[41]), while a shared environment only have a modest impact.[42] Twin studies even suggest that it's not living together that make people in a family similar; it mainly comes down to the shared genes. Fraternal twins, even if raised together, have been shown to be much less alike than identical twins reared apart.[43]

This is why it's so tricky when people try to get to know multiples, especially identicals such as us. We are indeed quite similar, at least on the surface, and if you're to sum us up in a few sentences or paragraphs, we end up sounding very much like the same person. Nuances are lost when you present someone shorthand, and especially if you resort to comparisons.

Yet, of course, the differences are there, at least if you dig a bit deeper and notice the smaller things, like a mole, a trademark gesture, or a more contagious laugh. You'll notice that one is an even more inclusive person who not only greets new people at work but also at the gym, that all three are sporty, but one is also an insane person who lives for a jump on the water on skis, and another thinks a *fifty-kilometer race* on New Year's Eve is good fun.

But describing my sisters in detail to you here would mean seeing them only in reference to each other. Inevitably I would need to qualify with "a bit more" and "a bit less" or resort to providing anecdote upon anecdote to get across how, for instance, both my sisters are caring but in slightly different ways, or how they're both killer story tellers yet Mariann might be more—and there it starts. I have to qualify Trude by saying "is probably less X." Sorry, I'm not going down that rabbit hole.

Back to my childhood memory of our names playing a game of musical chairs

Memory is a tricky thing. Neuroscientists say we should trust it less than most of us do. For a while that nugget was something for me to hold on to. At least until the one day I called my father to ask whether they could tell us apart as babies or not.

"It wasn't really a problem," he said. "When they—when you came home from the hospital then, there were these name tags on you. Bracelets around your ankles."

"The ones you kept on swapping?" my brother Stig said brightly, at our father's for a visit and, as if he could sniff comedy in waiting, not one to miss this particular conversation.

My father continued unperturbed. "Yes, we continued with the name tags. It was important that we didn't mess that up, especially when we were giving you food: that baby A would get food twice would of course be embarrassing."

There is no way they wouldn't have fed us properly. Even if they did miss one baby, said baby would have quickly made it clear more food was in order. Less obviously, and the question my father had yet to answer, were they able to tell us apart?

"No, not then. Because then there weren't these kind of characteristic traits about you. The first few years your faces and bodies changed a lot. So, in theory, some mix-ups could have happened, and I won't exclude the possibility that it may have happened."

He paused to think, while all I could think about was his word "then." When was "then"?—and "in theory"?! This was as far from "in theory" as I could imagine.

"The catastrophe would only have been if you would have needed essential medication."

True enough, but I could easily think of another complication. "Or if we were to have any issues with mistaken identity…?" I said cheerfully, intentionally letting the sentence trail off. My brother laughed while I don't think my father yet understood what I was getting at.

Clearly not having learnt my lesson, I continued probing. "Are we talking days, weeks—" and as a nice gesture, just to indicate that it really would be understandable if it had taken them a bit of time, I added the frankly ludicrous "—or months?"

"After about six months we had a good idea about who was whom."

Half a year?!

I must admit, I didn't see that coming.

Nor what he said next.

"Then we had to look closely. And if we had the three of you at a bit of a distance and you were jumping or twirling around, then it was very easy to mistake you. There were these kinds of small differences, like in the head shape, which made it possible for us to tell you apart. It was at a distance that it could be a bit difficult."

Thankfully, Stig jumped in.

"My story in all of this is that I'm the only one that has never been mistaken you. Ever. I have always been able to tell you apart. Whether it was from a distance or not. Because when Mum and Dad and Tord [our eldest brother] were mistaken, I found it hilarious. It proved that I was in fact the only one who always knew."

(Stig's actually wrong. Trude, Mariann, and I have never mistaken each other either. Might seem like an odd thing to say, but it only seems like that because, like my brother, you make the hiccup of thinking of us as *one*.)

"I'm sorry about this, Kari," my father said. "There weren't really that many funny episodes or anything I could come up with for your book. But I'll have a think if there are any funnier stories."

Was he kidding me?

"Are you kidding me?"

"What do you mean?" my father said, laughing heartily.

Well, for starters there was the entire thing about the name tags that could have fallen off.

"That you and Mariann may have swapped names?" he said, slowly, as if trying hard to understand what I could be getting at.

I nodded vigorously. "Yes! That was a major identity crisis. That meant that suddenly, I had become Mariann. My idea of identity at the time was my name!"

Mind you, by the time I was halfway through my reply, my father was laughing so hard I simply decided to push on.

"We were *mortified* when we asked, and you guys casually replied that 'yes, that might have happened.'"

My brother, almost as wholly amused as me, said: "Thirty-three percent chance you are, in fact, Kari!"

And then my father, still laughing: "But you can swap back again!" He eventually came up for air and gained his composure, "Yes, right."

I've yet to learn to read minds, even my sisters', but I'm quite confident that this was my father's way of ending this conversation.

Pitfalls to be aware of when bonding with babies you can't quite tell apart

As a child, my concern was whether I had suffered a name change or two, but, as an adult, the question that strikes me is, "How could this affect the parents of multiples?"

Fortunately for parents of multiples, psychologists have your back. Forming a secure attachment is a process, and one that takes time. Relationships are a continual process, and your relationship with your multiples is the same. Each is unique. And for that uniqueness to develop, you need to give it time. That's a message to take to heart, especially if you have identical multiples.

As we will see in chapter eight, researchers point to both an assimilation effect and a contrast effect for twins (it's damned if you do and damned if you don't—you're either made to be too similar to your co-twin, or your differences are overly emphasized).[44] Parents should be aware that you run the risk of exaggerating slight discrepancies or focusing on insignificant characteristics (like birth order or minute differences in birthweight) to distinguish between your multiples in order to develop a distinct relationship with each baby.[45,46,47] Interestingly and also immensely worrying from the perspective of a multiple, this often ends up creating *more* significant differences between the children as they grow.[48,49] Oh, and parents, be aware of the bias you may have towards one twin. Yes, we're talking favorites.

First, a few words to reassure you: your children might not notice. Recall the family with whom my sisters and I would spend many a weekend when we were little? (If not, flip back to chapter three.) In our mid-twenties the three of us visited, and one of the daughters in the house, by then a woman in her fifties, asked cautiously, "I'm just wondering, did you ever think much about the fact that Mariann was the favorite?" Mariann laughed; Trude and I shot each other a quick glance. *They had a favorite?!* "No, no," we reassured them on top of each other, yet each of us also thinking, *At least not until now!*

Studies suggest that if born an identical twin, you should really root hard for being the first-born or the first to be taken home from the hospital. This goes even if the difference in returning home is less than a week, as whoever comes homes first is reportedly perceived most favorably. Parents reported feeling closer to first-born identicals, who were seen to be easier to manage even if there was no difference in medical problems between the twins.[50,51]

What's important to note is that this Australian research did not reveal much favoritism based on birth order for same-sex fraternal pairs and no birth order differences in boy-girl pairs.[52] Pointing to our society's encouragement of individuality, Australian researcher David A. Hay says it is no surprise that parents and others look for something to distinguish their twins. Yet, here's the snag for us identicals: "If there is nothing obvious, they may focus on minor and otherwise irrelevant features."

Like who was the first-born.

In another Australian study that followed in the first one's heels, researcher Ann Bruce showed that the effects proved long-lasting. The way teachers perceived the twin's social adjustment at ages five to fifteen closely matched how the parents explained the parental preferences that had been established already when the twins were infants. Bruce writes, "Specifically, twins who left the hospital later than a co-twin were rated by teachers to be more withdrawn, depressed, and maladaptive toward peers than their co-twin."[53]

Yikes.

In another study of twenty-seven sets of identical female twins, parents' preference towards one twin increased from 63 percent in preschool to 85 percent during adolescence.[54] The parents' idea about who was 'better' had nothing to do with how the twins' performed on ability measures or how their teacher assessed their behavior.[55] And the variable that really mattered for parental bias? You might have guessed it already: Which twin had left hospital first after birth.[56]

Now, my first thought when I read about these studies was obviously, *What is up with Australians?!* My second was the same as any psychologist would ask: *Why?* Because regardless of actual differences between twins, parents tended to prefer one child over the other and this preference grew stronger as the children got older. Another study on this, also Australian, "suggested that the perceived differences are more likely differences in self-confidence potentially manufactured by parental expectations."[57] As one researcher noted, "Although emphasizing different characteristics may serve as a means of individual twin's identity formation, the problem with labeling is that the child tends to conform to the label whether it is just or not."[58] In plainer words, we're looking at a self-fulfilling prophecy.

A case study that illustrates the issue with self-fulfilling prophecies: *He's this and he's that*

Here's an interesting study that neatly illustrates the strong social environments in which we all operate: in a study of 30 sets of young Italian twins, the children often unexpectedly switched the roles assigned to them. As two mothers of identical twins put it, "It's incredible. He has become the other one!" and "Extraordinary! They are interchangeable!"[59]

While genes may have played a part, with one simply catching up (so to speak), study author Alessandra Piontelli notes another reason: those around had already mapped the twin's personalities. The twins had been assigned different labels and roles, of which identicals ended up with the more "clear-cut, rigid and oversimplified"; none of those "[s]ubtle tones and half-measures"[60]. Instead, Piontelli says, "differences were taken to their extremes without taking into account any of their nuances, including undoubted similarities, which went to make up the distinct personalities of each twin."

She offers several examples, which—on reflection—make these identical twins appear more like chalk and cheese than, well, identical: "One twin was good, the other bad; one cuddly, the other independent; one sociable, the other shy; one always on the move, the other a thinker." Faced with rigid roles both twins often found difficult to accept, they simply put themselves into the other's shoes, enabling them to express different aspects of their temperaments. And yet, although I'd like to say kudos for the effort to the young twins, those around didn't respond by expanding the assigned boxes. Rather, they would simply swap the labels, recreating the original division.[61] *He's this and he's that.*

Although you might make some hiccups with names—use them and not 'the twins' or 'the triplets'. I find it telling that my father said it became easier to tell us apart as soon as they had named us. Also, the power of your very own name is the very reason most multiples will vehemently object to being called "the twin" or "the triplet." Not too long ago, I met a friend of the family, a now forty-eight-year-old fraternal twin, who reminded me that my parents always made great care to call us by our names.

"I remember your mum was really strict about that. That's good. We were always 'the twins'." She paused a bit and then added, "still are for everyone."

As a parent, you should make sure to skip the label 'the twins' or 'the triplets' that groups your children with their siblings and rather use the names that go with the unique, individual little people. When you do list their names, make sure you change the order from time to time. You might not notice yourself, but you can bet that the child that always comes last does. Or, if your children are of the same gender, mix it up at times and say "the girls" or "the boys" instead. If they have older siblings, say "the youngest ones." You get the idea.

Because outside that free zone you've now established, very many will reach for "the twins" or "the triplets" when addressing your children rather than list two or three names.

Parents, rest assured—you have time

Your children will be none the wiser and feel no different about your warmth, kisses and cuddles whether you think of them as baby A, B, C, or even as D, E, F, or G…

Forming an individual bond with each child means you need to see them each as individuals and not merely as a group. And the secret to getting to know each of them as a single, special person? Spending time alone with each baby. It's what psychologist Joan A. Friedman, also a mother of twins, spells out in her thought-provoking book *Emotionally Healthy Twins: A New Philosophy for Parenting Two Unique Children*: "The best way to begin to establish a secure connection with each baby is to find out what your baby is like away from, and not in comparison with, her sibling." But also, she says, you might need it just as much as your children. In Friedman's own experience and also that of her clients, spending alone time with just one baby "helped to create a necessary bond between parent and child and enabled parents to feel that they were providing each child with what they needed most – exclusive attention from mom or dad."[62] It's about putting in some minutes here and there of getting to focus on just one exclusively – and about not feeling that you need to rush to characterize them.[63]

Because the only result you earn by rushing is running the risk of assigning personality traits—too early. So, the next time your neighbor asks who's the funny one, who's the cry baby, and who will become the next prime minister, simply smile and laugh and say, "Who knows. I can't tell them apart yet!" Chances are your neighbor will laugh, and you won't to have to lie.

As an adult I'm fine with the idea that my name might have played a bit of musical chairs. Because when the music stopped, and someone tried to figure out who I was, it was based on the shape of my head. I wasn't the funny one, the laid-back one, or the sweet one.

Coming back to *Wonderland*, Alice eventually found her way back to her true size and self. "'That *was* a narrow escape!' said Alice, a good deal frightened at the sudden change, but very glad to find herself still in existence".[64] She wasn't Ada, nor Mabel, but Alice.

Sure, I might be Trude. I might be Mariann. But, if nothing else, I know that you can grow into a name. I'll stick with Kari.

Lastly, a few practical tips on keeping tabs of those names:

- Name tags, friendship bracelets or cotton strands in different colors around their ankles or a wrist
- Search for birthmarks or characteristics like a freckle, different head shape, etc.
- Color-coordinate or keep them dressed in "their" color
- Paint a toenail on each in different colors
- Write their initial on the bottom of their feet
- Write their initial on the diaper—keep two or three stacks, depending on the numbers you need to keep count of

…and what not to do:

- Don't tell them their name tags continuously fell off

CHAPTER 5

Stubborn twin myths and what to tell your children

There are a lot of terrific bits of nonsense surrounding twins. On top of the list is the view that being an identical multiple is the Holy Grail of relationships, leaving society looking foggy-eyed at identicals and many fraternals feeling shafted. Yet, the worlds of fraternals and identicals largely overlap and it's the nuances of what it's like to be a multiple, the ones we normally don't tell people about, that matter and that all twins and triplets should know about. And the way to tell young multiples is through a Harry Potter-marathon with lots of popcorn and stories of real twins versus fictional ones.

Already more than sixty years ago, American psychoanalyst Dorothy Burlingham called the bond between twins "the closest tie between two people."[65] Society's fascination with twins, she argued, develops when we're young, when we're seeking to cope with separateness from our parents. Our longing for a twin is the fantasy of a mirror image, someone who would be capable of deep, intuitive, empathetic understanding, the perfect kind of closeness, an untroubled and unchanging relationship.[66]

That very fantasy is the reason why, if you were to ask one of us what it's like to be a multiple, we answer on autopilot.

"I grew up with my two best friends," we say with a smile. *Aaah*, their eyes say. "Triplet bliss!"

Nothing surprising there. Nods and smiles all around.

In my late teens, I sometimes used the fact that I was a triplet as a nifty party trick. Whenever I wanted to bask in attention or speed up a slow group conversation, I'd let it slip into conversation. It didn't even have to be subtle. "I'm actually an identical triplet." A sure-fire way to steer all conversation to me: "*Wow! I've always wanted to be a twin*", "*That must be so cool*", "*Fantastic, I've never met a triplet before. And an identical triplet! What's that like?*"

It's a conversation that self-selects. We stick to the twin fantasy, knowing well that people dream of having a twin, and that offering any nuance makes us sound either ungrateful or simply inept at taking advantage of the perceived winning hand dealt us at birth. Or, worse yet, it might lead us to inadvertently criticize our siblings. So, multiples answer yes, it's bloody marvelous, thank you very much.

Stereotypes of twins fit into one of two categories: cool or creepy

Let's have a look at some of the stereotypes of twins. Ideas about twins have abounded since the ancient Greeks, but laziness over the centuries means we can nip directly into popular culture to find the dominant themes.

In one incarnation, twins are inseparable best friends, a double act who dress alike, look alike, and share everything, including sentences. Prime contenders are the Weasley twins, the prankster duo in Harry Potter who have their own joke shop, Weasley's Wizard Wheezes, which sells trick wands, flying toy cars, and nose-biting teacups! Find me a child who doesn't want a sidekick like that.

But then there's also the freaky, creepy, spooky, evil, dysfunctional twins that can't function without the other or who are fierce rivals. It's the Grady twins in the hallway from *The Shining*, the albino, dreadlocked twins in *The Matrix*, and Marge Simpsons' sisters Selma and Patty, who never separate or go on to form other adult relationships. It's also Sherri and Terri in the Simpsons, who retreat into their own twin language and struggle to share each other; when Bart Simpson becomes Terri's boyfriend, not only is Sherri unhappy without her twin sister, all the other girls find it weird to hang out with just one twin and give her the cold shoulder.

Before we go on, I need to spell out the similarities in the above: The twins' all appear or are best kept together, and let's not forget, they're all *identical* twins.

Being a multiple is a minefield—you need get it *right*. And getting it right means being an *identical* multiple

The pervading idea of what a twin is in our culture is *an identical twin*. The extraordinary has become the norm. (Quite tactless, the French call fraternal twins 'faux jumeaux', meaning false twins. Identical twins are the 'vrais jumeaux', real twins.)

Every year, there's a humongous gathering of about 3000 sets of twins at the Twins Day festival in Twinsburg, Ohio. (No,

I'm not making this up. I even looked it up to check: Twinsburg is an actual place, a small Midwestern city, where a set of inseparable identical twins in the early 1800s persuaded the other residents to change the settlement's name from Millsville to Twinsburg by offering land for a public square and money toward starting a school. And we multiples wonder why people sometimes think we're weird...). In an article about the festival, a journalist concluded that a strong inferiority complex lurks in the world of twins. Amid identicals dressed similarly from head to toe, a fraternal twin confides, "I feel shafted here because everybody looks the same." His brother agrees, "Yeah, we're the redheaded stepchild here, the fraternals." Other fraternals speak of feeling cheated by the fact that they weren't identical. "We never got to be that set of twins that [fooled teachers] and switched around in class." A mother of fraternal twins says it is a caste system, with identicals on top of the hierarchy.[67]

A small pause here to tell any fraternal twins reading this: the craving for changing places in a classroom quickly passes. When we did it, the teachers rarely noticed and eventually we tired of the game, or one of our classmates would raise a little arm, asking, "Do you notice anything different?"

"No," the teacher would reply, scanning the classroom.

"Trude, Kari, and Mariann have swapped places," a fairly in-unison reply would come from our classmates. While the other children found it hilarious that the teachers couldn't tell, for many years I suspected their casual shrug as a reply was an attempt to make the game less exciting. Only as an adult do I realize that it probably didn't matter all that much if Trude sat where Mariann or I should have been sitting.

Also, here's a conversation our mother had with our teacher who'd been seeing us every day when we were twelve. "It's a pity that Trude's now getting glasses as well. She was so easy to tell apart." Mum looked at him slightly perplexed, not sure at first whether to take him seriously.

"Trude's had glasses for two years," she replied. "It's Mari-ann that's getting glasses now." *Potayto, potahto.*

Anyways. Shortly after reading about Twinsburg, I came across the website of an Australian documentary on twins. Mind you, identical twins, as fraternal twins wouldn't make compelling TV or enable introductions like this: "What's it like to grow up with another you? To share, not only your face but maybe also your thoughts, your dreams and even your pain? That's a question only identical twins can answer."[68] (*Share our thoughts, our dreams, our pain*? Seriously?) While fraternals didn't appear in the documentary, many had left comments on the website, including this question: Why is there no interest in fraternal twins?

As one fraternal twin wrote: "I am a fraternal twin and unfortunately feel that fraternal twins are somewhat less interesting. Fraternal twin girls are very rare, and my sister and I are very close. But we are very different people and I find that just as special. I often struggle to maintain an identity as a twin because we 'don't look the same.'"

Want the truth?

None of this surprised me. The reality is, of course, that we identicals are fully aware of the additional brownie points that come our way due to our sameness. To illustrate, here's a bit from a memoir by American identical twin Abigail Pobgrebin. At one point she decides she needs to know for sure that she is in fact an identical twin. (Or, more likely, her editor compelled her, saying it makes for highly entertaining reading.)

As she opens the email from the lab with the DNA results, Pobgrebin says her heart leaps. She's always felt, she writes, that her closeness with her sister is authenticated by their sameness. Then (as if French), she adds: "I also worried that after a lifetime of presenting ourselves as the genuine article, we'd be exposed as fake."[69] Identical twins have a dirty secret, Pobgrebin claims: "We all feel slightly superior to the fraternal brand. We're the gold standard: rarer, more identifiable, more mysterious. We happen only by accident."[70]

Well, here's a dirty secret from an identical triplet. As a child, I often thought of twins, whether identical or fraternal, as a bit like vanilla yoghurt: nice, but plain. As far as I was concerned, twins weren't even part of the same category as my sisters and I; there were just two of them.

Everywhere I looked, there were twins, both identical and fraternal, but hardly ever any triplets, and whenever I replied to the question of whether we were twins with "No, we're triplets, but the third's not here," it would immediately be confirmed that I belonged to a vastly superior breed of multiples. *Wow, I've met twins before, but never triplets! That is amazing!* Other triplets appear to have picked up on the same. Here's a quote from an interview with 60-year old identical triplets: "Robert is the youngest; he says, "Without me, they were just twins. I made them what they are: triplets."[71]

Yet, here's another secret: there were times, growing up, I wished I was a fraternal twin. It just seemed a whole lot easier.

A set of fraternal twins lived next to my aunt. They would often come around when we visited, and from my position in the kitchen, watching them approach the door, ring that doorbell, and then immediately be identified by their names, it seemed like these two girls had a pretty sweet deal. As far as I was concerned, fraternals had a twinship blissfully hidden from everyone else. They had each other but none of the negatives.

Fraternal, identical, twin, triplet? Our worlds largely overlap

It's what I've increasingly realized as an adult. All twins are impacted by stubborn, pesky myths about twinship and triplethood.

Here is a story to illustrate. I recently learned that one of my colleagues is a twin. She mentioned it casually, taking me by surprise, probably because most people who know me well also know that I am a triplet or at least that I have two sisters. My colleague and I had known each other for two years, and she had never even mentioned having a sister.

"I didn't know you were a twin," I said.

"*Yeesss*," she said slowly, "but we're not *that* kind of twins. We're fraternal, so not quite like that." But when she told her twin story, it sounded a lot like a story many identical twins could tell.

Today, the sisters are close and speak daily. But, it had been painful being a twin when little, she said. "I wanted people to see *me*. That I was *only* me." She and her sister didn't look anything alike, weren't that close, and her main memory from a twinned childhood was a sister who always tried to tag along with her and her friends. They were treated similarly growing up, she said, and shared classmates until they were thirteen. "Then I got my own class and that was fantastic!"

She asked if I remembered how children at school used to dress up like twins to show to the world that they were best friends; I did remember. To "do" twins properly, you dressed the same and tried to be as similar as possible. My colleague remembered even more twin fascination within the concept of pen pals, which were all the rage in the '80s when we grew up. "I remember that people wanted a pen pal who was born on the same day so that they could pretend that they were twins. I remember rolling my eyes and thinking, *Oh my god, why in the world would they want to do that?*"

A bespoke Harry Potter-marathon to help your children bear conflicting feelings about being a multiple

While myths take a long time to shift, we all have a chance to call out our own preconceptions about multiples. If you're a parent of multiples, focus on uniqueness and not the notion of your twins as a rare, mysterious gold standard—but on each of them, individually. And, to help your children more easily bear whatever feelings they have about being a twin, I recommend a Harry Potter-marathon accompanied by ~~a large bowl of popcorn~~ separate buckets of popcorn, alongside the story of the Weasley twins versus the actors who portrayed them. So, plonk your children down in front of the TV and pause the Harry Potter-marathon whenever you spot one of the myriad twin clichés—be it when the Weasley's speak on top of each other, are referred to as 'the twins', appear in identical clothing or swap places—in order to tell them about these twins in real life and as many other stories from this book needed to help them realize that the grass isn't necessarily greener and that most twins portrayed on TV is just that, TV. Made up.

You see, in an interview after the film series ended, actors Oliver and James Phelps shared a more universal twin story than the Weasley's: how annoying it is to be treated as a unit rather than as individuals, how they'd always fought against dressing the same, and how when little, the boys would ignore anyone who referred to them as "the twins."[72]

While obviously grateful for their roles, the two said it felt like a step backwards to be known as the twins again, now on a global scale. During the last few years at secondary school, they'd carefully carved out their own identities, been apart for the first time and made their own friends.[73] As James Phelps put it, "I know people don't mean to be insulting, and I know that some twins enjoy being seen as twins, but we're at the other end of the scale."[74]

Your multiples need to know that. Being a twin or triplet is not always what it's cracked up to be, and that is perfectly fine.

Do you recall the potential fourth and the sister Mariann, Trude and I could have ended up with? (If not, shuffle the pages back to chapter one). In my mind, she would have been completely different from Trude and Mariann. When I was annoyed with them and was wishing for them to be far away, I at times found myself wishing I had my third sister next to me instead. She'd be the perfect playmate who'd always be on my side and would always agree with me. She'd be more like me than these other two.

What I didn't know then but do now is that my sisters had similar thoughts. Trude says cheerfully, "As a child, I figured that the one who didn't make it had to be my person, because these two others were much stupider than me. I always assumed she would have been incredibly cool. And whenever we played games that really should have been between four people, I remember thinking, *Oh, why couldn't she have made it!* It was a fairly practical way of thinking about it. But I remember it well: my person wasn't there."

So, there we were, identical multiples dreaming of, well—how to put it?—the perfect twin, the one who'd be just like ourselves, but also the one who doesn't exist, because thankfully, we're all—even us identical multiples—unique.

Twin myths matter when you realize first as an adult that you're a multiple

Unfortunately, more people out there know the twin story of Fred and George Weasley than the one of Oliver and James Phelps. And many of those would happily sign up to get their very own sidekick.

In his book *Twins: And What They Tell Us About Who We Are*, journalist Lawrence Wright says stories of reunited twins are perhaps so compelling due to the implicit suggestion that it could happen to anyone:

"It feeds the common fantasy that any one of us might have a clone, a doppelgänger; someone who is not only a human mirror but also an ideal companion; someone who understands me perfectly, almost perfectly, because he is me, almost me."[75]

I'm certain that most, it not all, multiples who's grown up as one would balk at descriptions like "he is me, almost me." But, how do you react if you've lived all your life with mere ideas about what it's like to be a twin, and then suddenly you find yourself to be one?

As I guess has happened to many a multiple, several friends this year sent me links, asking whether I'd seen the news articles about *Three Identical Strangers*. The documentary tells the story of identical triplets Bobby Shafran, Eddy Galland, and David Kellman, who were separated at birth only to be reunited at age 19. The boys were part of a secret, twisted study, along with a dozen more sets of identical siblings, all split up and adopted out to separate families with different socioeconomic backgrounds. In their childhood years, researchers came to the adopted children's homes in the aim of studying the effects of nature and nurture. The families were never told that their child had identical sibling(s) and what the true intentions of the research was.

The documentary details the initial honeymoon period for the reunited trio, in which they played up similarities, which fed both the media and talk show audiences, and served as wish-fulfilment for themselves. In an interview, David Kellman says the brothers were sort of falling in love. "It was, 'You like this thing? I love that!' There was definitely a desire to like the same things and to be the same."[76]

His brother Bobby Shafran agrees. "We found the ways we were alike and we emphasized them."[77]

Director Tim Wardle points to the obsession with identicals going back to Romulus and Remus, saying, "And the siblings wanted to believe that they were similar, too. It's that thing where you fall in love with someone for the first time, you try and find everything you have in common. 'Oh my God, we like the same music!' But you sort of tone down the differences."[78]

At first, the brothers did cameos on *Cheers* and in *Desperately Seeking Susan* (ogling Madonna), moved into a bachelor pad in Queens together, and capitalized on the twin frenzy with their own steakhouse in Soho, New York. It was called, of course, "Triplets."[79]

I know the pain that comes with spoilers, so I'll keep mostly mum about what follows and only share this: At the end of the documentary, their relationship had severely cooled, with the brothers appearing, in the words of one film critic, "less like siblings, more like slightly uneasy acquaintances".[80] It was a fallout that didn't come as a surprise to the director. While the twins who took part in the study instantly connected upon reuniting, most of the estranged twins struggled to maintain their relationships:

> *One of the fascinating things we learnt was a lot of the other people in the study, the ones that we know about that aren't in the film that we spoke to, when they first met after being reunited with their twin they were incredibly close and had this close relationship.*
>
> *But almost all of them have fallen out since. It is almost as if the human brain can't cope with meeting a clone of yourself in the 20s or 30s. They just didn't have the experience of growing up together to work out all of their issues. It is hard to do it later in life.*[81]

There are levels to this story I can't relate to, more specifically the "sliding doors" element—the question of what could have happened to me if I was brought up in another family altogether, unaware that I was a multiple. What I can relate to are the issues that can arise when navigating one's own and others' expectations of a twin relationship.

Yet, it's all taken up a few notches compared to my own experience as a multiple. It's hard to fathom what it's like to be hurled into fame based on similarity with one or two others as an adult, facing the comparisons and a sudden push for sameness with strangers and perhaps also expecting that easy intimacy that supposedly comes with being twins.

Because what then when these strangers turn out to be mere people, that don't always display the promised deep connection, and you realize that the bond is not just down to genes but something that requires shared experiences and intimacy over time to build? Then pile on top of that expectations from both you and the world that these others are like you, which may make their very quirks, flaws, and shortcomings much more apparent—to you.

Here is an excerpt from an interview with another set of multiples that unknowingly took part in the same study, also separated and adopted to different families at birth:

> Interviewer: But there were dark elements: What would it be like to confront an alternate version of you?
>
> Paula: In the beginning, we saw each other's mannerisms as more intense, sometimes more irritating, than our own. At times, it's like, I already know what you're going to say, why even talk—
>
> Elyse: But on the flip side, sometimes we don't know. And then it's like, How could you not understand? You should read my mind![82]

Here's another spoiler though from the world of multiples, courtesy of yours truly: Identical multiples can't read each other's minds.

What about that famed twin bond then? Isn't it true? It is, but again, nuance matters.

In her book, *'Entwined Lives: Twins and What They Tell Us About Human Behavior'*, twin researcher, fraternal twin and evolutionary psychologist Nancy Segal includes the chapter 'Friendship Extraordinaire: Twins' Special Relationship'. She starts the chapter with two opening quotes:

- "My boys were thrilled to learn that they are definitely identical twins. Why, I don't really know, but it is a big deal to them." – A mother of twins
- "They (identical twin brothers) are more important to each other than I am to either of them" – A nonidentical male triplet with identical twin brothers

Not surprising, Segal says. Instead, this is simply consistent with how identicals and fraternal twins act towards each other. The closer social bonds, she argues, come down to biology, which affects how we behave towards one another. In other words, the closer the gene pool, the closer social bonds. A few pages on, Dorothy Burlingham and her take on the identical twin bond as the "closest tie between two people" appears. A theme, Segal says, that has been repeated in several analysis: "The view that one is and should be closer to the twin than to other siblings has been expressed more often by identical than by fraternal twins."

That may be so, but as I leafed through Segal's book I felt my skepticism growing. I have a hard time believing that two young boys' thrilled reaction at being identicals comes down to genes. I think it's safe to say that we're faced with something that smacks of social expectations. Society looks awe-fogged at identical twins. Not so much at fraternal twins.

There are also many researchers who believe there's more than genes in the pudding. One of them is American psychologist and identical twin Barbara Klein, who's one of the world's leading twin experts. She argues that contrary to the genetic bond, it's the quality of parenting that is crucial for the twin bond. While Klein never experienced the harmonious twin relationship herself, years of academic research and clinical work with adult twins led her to the pattern that would. Not surprising, this is the twin bond she describes as 'individual identity twins', which comes about when "parents respond to real individual differences between their twin children and encourage them to function as individuals." She writes, "Twins who were treated as individuals growing up maintained a close bond to one another, as well as their independence, throughout their lives."[83]

Let's pause for a second here. Like mine is right now, any book on multiples will inevitably be knee-deep in the nature versus nurture debate. I don't have the full story on twin research and I don't intend to strike a clear conclusion on topics where psychologists are hotly divided in their theories. Like most psychological theories, closeness between twins and triplets can't be proven in a lab. There are no independently verifiable facts. But, there are numerous reasons to err on the side of caution. It's safer to firmly believe we are receiving input, so we can deal with that.

Because closest bond between two or three people or not, what I seek to convey in this book is that it's the nuances, the ones we normally don't tell people about, that matter. It's what becomes apparent when Dorothy Burlingham's quote is placed in its proper context.

Because what most books on twins fail to tell you alongside her famous quote is that Burlingham was also the first to happily debunk the twin fantasy. In her 1952 case study of three sets of identical twins, she continued typing until none of her readers would longer believe it would simply be wonderful to have a look-alike. At the time, twins were perceived as seamlessly interchangeable or as possessing a mysterious bond. And, in the fantasy, according to Burlingham, the bond between twins was imagined as an untroubled and unchanging one.

However, as the interview with the Phelps brothers reveals, fiction and reality are often quite different. In the same manner, the twins Burlingham studied struggled with conflicting feelings around the need for independence and the fear of separation. Here's a conversation between a duo she studied:

Nearly four-year-old Mary to Madge: "Madge, you're a twin."

Madge: "No I'm not, I'm Madge."[84]

I like Madge.

Now, my sisters both chuckled at this point when they read a draft of this chapter.

"I like Madge too," they both replied.

My husband, whom I also bribed into reading my drafts, wondered why I liked Madge, saying it wasn't obvious to him, but I think it is to anyone who's a multiple. It's what Madge, not even four years old, had already understood; she is first and foremost herself, she is *Madge*, and then maybe a twin as well.

Even if your multiples (at least today) think being a twin or a triplet is brilliant, still insist on telling them a few of these stories. They need to know that however they're feeling about being a multiple is perfectly fine, and that chances are at least some of those other 125 million living multiples in the world feel the same way.

What they do not need, however, is for you to push hard on the twin fantasy at home, the rest of the world is doing that just fine. For sure, let them be proud to be a multiple, but make sure they're even prouder of who they are.

Just the one.

Like Madge.

CHAPTER 6

The crash-course in dressing multiples

How to dress multiples, and the big take-home from this book, is easy to remember:

- **Rule #1: If it smacks of being gimmicky, don't do it.**
- **Rule #2: If it helps to distinguish, do so.**

I once went to an indoor soft-play session for under-fives in a large sports hall. Toward the end of the session all the parents formed a circle while our children bounced up and down in the middle to various songs we sang together, and during this I had a good fifteen minutes to observe a set of twins.

They were probably close to five in age, these two girls, and as identical looking as any twins I'd ever seen, and yet I didn't spot them at first. Their heights, bodies, faces, and whatever aspects beyond the control of the parents were similar, sure, but everything else was different. One had her curly hair in a ponytail, wore pink shoes, a pink top, and pink trousers. The other had a short haircut, her curls framing her face, and her clothes were not just a different color to her sister's—grey and purple—but entirely different in style.

As the session ended and parents rushed to get out, I wheeled my son's pram over to the woman who was busy putting shoes on the two little girls.

"Excuse me, are these your girls?"

"Yes, they're twins," she said automatically, barely looking up from lacing on the shoes.

"I'm an identical triplet," I said, "and I just wanted to tell you how amazing it is that you made them look so different."

"Oh." She stood up, shoe in hand, looking at me. Admittedly, she looked a bit puzzled, so I figured I should go on.

"You've done so much to make them look different. I just wanted to say that I think you're doing a wonderful, wonderful job."

She looked like she was about to cry, so I gave her shoulder a gentle squeeze and figured I should end the conversation before I teared up too.

"Anyways, I'm going to let you get back to your girls. I just wanted to let you know that I noticed your massive effort and I think you're amazing."

"Thank you," she said, gave it a little pause, and then repeated, "Thank you, thank you, thank you."

A friend of mine, who had also been at the soft play, waited for me outside. I apologized for keeping her waiting, saying that I had stopped to speak with the mother of the twins.

"There were twins in there? I didn't see them."

Exactly.

You want to make it *easier* for people to distinguish multiples, not *harder*

"To each their own," I once read on a forum for parents of triplets. The discussion went back and forth on whether to dress the children alike or not, whether it was still okay to match them, whether to assign colors, and would the children be bothered by wearing a name tag?

On this one, I'm certain where I stand: it's *not* to each their own.

Common sense will help you a long way here. You can make choices that makes it easier for your children to be multiples, whether they're fraternal or identical; if you have identicals, it's obviously especially important. But, even if your multiples aren't identical or even similar-looking, you don't want to add layers of confusion.

In a manual for professionals working with multiples, Pat Preedy, a UK education expert who has specialized in twins, says adults frequently perceive twins, triplets, and quadruplets as a natural unit. She writes: "Just knowing that the children are multiples seems to affect the memory, so that identifying them as individuals and calling them by their names becomes an impossibility."[85] And here's why you shouldn't add to the confusion: "If this perception is reinforced by the parents and the children themselves then the teacher is likely to perceive and treat the multiples as one, expecting the same outcomes from each. Even their friends may fail to differentiate, playing with either or both as they were one."[86]

I ran Preedy's research past my cousins, fifteen-year-old fraternal male twins: one tall, one short; one blonde, one brown-haired; both always dressed differently. They were as clear in their conclusion as she was: "Makes perfect sense!"

As it turns out, fraternals also frequently end up being called the wrong name. My cousins let me in on a story of a recent substitute teacher: "For the first few lessons, she had no problem at all telling us apart and using the right name. But then someone told her we were twins, and then she kept getting our names wrong. I thought she'd gone bonkers, but I get it now."

The reasons parents want to dress multiples the same or match them are wholly understandable

I once read about a triplet mother who'd been to a local shop with her fraternal triplets and their older brother. Unlike the standard looks of curiosity, encouragement, or even sympathy, that day she noted an atmosphere of annoyance as she struggled to keep the children from running about and colliding with supermarket trolleys. She felt like a hot mess. The reason, she guessed, was that her children were dressed differently that day.

Indeed. It's what parents of multiples know well and what researcher Alessandra Piontelli found when she followed thirty sets of twins from pregnancy to early childhood. Parents basked in reflected glory when their twins were around, and few resisted the temptation of the limelight. And if the maximum attention was to be achieved, twinning had to be maximized.[87]

Parents' protests at the attention were, however, feeble. Not least, Piontelli says, because few of them avoided using any of the "elementary Gestalt stratagems".[88] No worries, I looked it up. Gestalt is a psychology term about theories of visual perception. One of them is 'similarity', which means that people perceive objects that look similar as a group or pattern.[89] In other words, if your multiples sport the same haircut or wear the same or similar clothes, you're not as a parent lending a hand to others, who in the face of so much similarity will see these two or three as a unit. As Piontelli notes, somewhat dryly: "If two people want to pass unnoticed, wearing different, plain clothes is unquestionably a good start." Yet, most of the parents dressed the twins alike.[90] And the effect? Even close relatives and caregivers gave a pass at distinguishing the identical twins when dressed alike, rather pointing out in an amused tone that the twins could no longer be told apart.[91]

While psychologists say no, I say bring on the sunshine from time to time

Psychologist and identical twin Barbara Klein is the harshest critic I've found on the issue of dressing twins the same. It's a cop-out parenting strategy, as far as she's concerned. Klein quotes a fictitious mother who says, "I will just dress the twins alike and make the most of being the mother of multiples. The attention I get from my children will make up for the troubles of raising them."[92] Her argument takes a brief stop at "ridiculous attitude" and "sure-fire mistake"[93] before she ends with, "Encouraging any kind of narcissistic gain—such as special attention from onlookers—is totally counterproductive to the development of individuality. Mental health professionals need to look at why parents are using their twin children as narcissistic extensions."[94] *Ouch.*

Yet, however much I agree with Klein's take on dressing multiples differently, it also makes me think of a conversation I had with my father about this, in which he said, "We had the humanist philosophy that it was a matter of three individual human beings, that they had to be allowed—although they are identical and although they live in the same family—to develop differently as well. You weren't 'the triplets' at home. You were Kari, Mariann, and Trude."

He continued, "Then you may say that this was somehow colliding with the fact that you were dressed alike as small children all the time, and that may have had a bit to do with status and pride, and perhaps in particular for Mum. It is obvious that when we went outside with three identically dressed girls, wearing sweaters and jackets that Mum had sewed, a bit of sunshine fell on the entire family. So that might have been a contributing cause, even though Mum often said that the reason was that it was more practical and easier to dress you alike."

My take is that yes, bring on the sunshine from time to time. If there is any way your twins or triplets may brighten up the first year, making it slightly peachier by just being astonishingly similar, and you and everyone around you find that to be incredibly cute, then I say go for it. As I see it, it's like the Internet's advice of drawing a moustache on a colicky infant. It doesn't bother the infant, and it brightens up the parents' day.

Parents don't let your children decide whether to dress the same

The truth is, I'm skeptical when parents of multiples say their children choose to dress alike or say they leave it entirely up to their children to make the decision. In an online forum for parents of triplets, a mother said she had taken her eight-year-old girls to the doctor. It was implied to them, she wrote, that since they dressed the same (and here she added in brackets "their choice"), they were not individuals. One of the girls had replied, "Oh, we are individuals. We know who we are, that's why we have different names!" And then the mother summed it up. "You have to love kids... they are honest and to the point." True. But the bigger point here is this: their world may not see it that way, and that world gives them input. While the children may know in their hearts that they're distinct, and their parents may be baffled when others can't tell their clearly distinct children apart, the reality is that the rest of the world clings to the twin myth and often treats them as the same.

Should you really let children decide something that is so important, something that might lead people to see them as a group rather than as individuals? Children don't always know what's best for them, and they don't make choices in a vacuum. It doesn't take many occasions of being dressed alike to realize that it ups your cuteness.

As adolescence happens, twins want to dress differently

Now, clothes, whether the same or different, weren't really an issue for my sisters and I until we hit adolescence. But then, as we headed down the twin paths of becoming independent and developing individuality, we were suddenly very much aware that clothes formed part of the challenge. Studies of twins reveal the same.[95]

In conversations with psychologist Barbara Klein, close to 60 adult twins speaking about their teenage years said that while the sharing of clothes continued, they were now careful to not be seen wearing the same clothes at the same time. "In fact", Klein notes, "most twins at this time in their lives tried to develop new styles for themselves that made them feel like they were very distinct individuals. For example, one twin might select a preppie style, whereas her sister chose a more bohemian style."[96]

Unfortunately, we were fierce defenders of all things equal, which in our world meant "identical." That translated into separate wardrobes, but the clothes within each were pretty much identical to the others'. (For some reason our underwear drawer remained shared, one of those things that should be on the list "You know you're a multiple if...") Obviously a recipe for disaster when you're intent on *not* dressing the same.

Our brother Stig found it hilarious. "What I remember most about the thing about dressing alike, is that at one point in time it changed. And it became incredibly important for you to not dress alike. I remember finding it highly entertaining in the morning when two had put on the same outfit and you had a massive argument about who needed to change."

Yet, for cloned wardrobes and non-identical outfits to work, multiples need cooperative siblings. An identical twin once told me he'd tried the same negotiation as us in the mornings with little effect. Looking into the cloned wardrobe that was his own, he'd announce with all the authority he could muster, "This is *my* sweater for today." His brother would shrug and say, "I don't care. If you mind, then *you* change." And his brother pulled out the very same sweater; definitely *his* for the day. It worked like a charm every day. Unwilling to dress alike and unable to call his brother's bluff, my friend found himself changing every time his brother opted for the same clothes.

Or maybe the brother wasn't bluffing. To my surprise, Mariann has a different take on this than Trude and I, saying, "When it comes to clothes, I think it's okay with a bit of a mix. When we went to a family gathering or a party, I think it was fine that we often had similar or identical clothes. It is special to be a multiple, and the children should be allowed to experience that as well. To get that attention. I remember I got annoyed at the ones who thought we looked different from each other, because yes, we did look different, but we were much more similar than other siblings. So, in a way I wanted that unity, be associated as one of us three, at the same time as I wanted to be just me. It's a difficult thing, because you want to be part of the group at the same time as you'd like to be yourself."

"But don't you remember the identical wardrobes and quarrelling?" I ask her.

"No," she replies. "Who knows, maybe I was always first and had my pick, because I don't remember it like that. I think Trude and you were more concerned about clothes and these things that I were—and are now."

Mariann continues, "It might be okay for parents to know that this might be more important for some of their children than others. It's of course not one rule that's valid. Parents need to follow their instincts regarding what's right for their children and their unique situation. I remember some of the issues with the clothing, now that you mention it, but that's perhaps because I rather remember that you guys have spoken about it. Did I just mess up your entire book? *Ha ha ha.*"

No, it's all good. I like to think that it proves the point. Sometimes it's delightful to bask in that additional attention. That's why I've taken it upon myself to high-five any parents that take steps to differentiate their twins.

When parents give up on the twin stardust, we need to be there to cheer them on. If you're in doubt whether the children you've encountered are multiples or not, take the chance. Parents who rarely get the question might be amused, and if they're indeed parents of multiples they're veterans in answering questions from strangers. But, when the latter parents brace themselves for a snowstorm of questions, that's your cue for the follow-up champagne toast. Tell them you noticed how they've sought to differentiate the children. The parents who try so hard to make each of their children stand out on their own need to know that it works. We see it. We see *them*. They're different.

As one parent of identical twins (herself a fraternal twin!) told me, the stranger who one day told her it was great that she dressed her twins differently: "Thanks, but it never even occurred to me to dress them identically. Why would I? They're different people."

Tips on how to differentiate multiples visually

Although nothing is fail-safe, parents of multiples need to do something. Between us three, as children, we had a mole and two scars—rather useless in the grand scheme of things. Even people who knew to be on the lookout for a mole at times forgot which girl it belonged to. There was a need for more striking clues as to who was who. Here are therefore a few ideas, most of them tried and tested:

1. Put a name or an initial on it

One of my husband's favorite stories from my childhood is from kindergarten: a puzzled new assistant stands facing a trio of little ones persistently holding out their little fists, waiting patiently by the entrance; eventually, another adult walks by and offers an explanation: "Oh, they're just waiting for their initials!

I don't recall having an initial written on my hand in kindergarten, but I do recall what I wore a few years later as I ran about in gym class at the age of six: a red leotard bearing the largest "K" I have ever worn, an initial some thirty centimeters high in neon-pink adhesive gel, on both the front and back.

As we got older, subtler things were attempted. There were the white woolen hats with our name spelled across the front in red. We also had several wooden brooches, painted purple, pink, or blue, with small flowers dotting the edges and our initials or names written across them. I still have them in a wooden box at home, little maps to who I was, making it possible for people to start a conversation with, "Hi Kari!" rather than "Which one are you?"

2. Different haircuts or hairstyles

Different haircuts is probably the best method (as long as you can get your children to agree), but you can also go far with simply different hairstyles. When we were little, our mother brushed and fixed our hair every morning. It paid off to be first: you got to choose what you wanted, as we all had to have different hairdos to help people tell us apart. If one sister had chosen a ponytail, then your wish for a ponytail would only happen if you also agreed to let it transition into a braid. More importantly, you didn't want to go after two others had sat wincing and squirming in the hair-chair. Mum's patience was running thin by then.

You can also opt for different hair-lengths, but I feel a bit ashamed to suggest that. At the age of ten, when I should have known better, I committed a triplet faux pas and spent weeks nagging my mother to cut my quite long hair shorter. I must have been persuasive, because both my sisters thought it was an excellent idea and wanted in on it too. I don't remember this, but apparently, I let both cut their hair short before I changed my mind. It didn't look that good after all.

3. Assign colors

In many ways this can be a good system. Parents report that their children quickly take to "their" color by deeming it a favorite, and you avoid a lot of arguments over whose sweater is whose. It also makes it possible to always make out who's who in photos. Your children might want a say in which Paw Patrol or Teletubby they are about to become though, so it might be best to put off allocating colors until they are old enough to choose for themselves. As well, one small downside I heard from a triplet mother is that other children might end up calling them "the green one, the blue one and the red one."

There are also variations at play here. Some parents go for different-colored shirts or trousers, while others try a more downplayed version and make sure that the shoes or even just the shoelaces are different colors.

4. Different clothes or shoes altogether

Assigning completely different clothes seems like a good way to go, but, if you run into a discussion with your duo or trio, all of whom would like that very sweater or cap, then you might want to go down the route of parents who never allow their children to get identical shoes but the same clothes in different colors.

5. Cheat sheets

When we were little our parents told their closest friends and our neighbors about characteristics that made it easier to tell us apart. I know some genius triplet parents who took this a notch farther by writing out proper cheat sheets to distribute to friends, neighbors, and teachers.

As with most good ideas, it's simple and easy to do: divide a piece of paper into three columns and jot down details enabling others to tell who's who. Are there any moles, freckles, or birthmarks? Differences in head shape? Gaps in teeth? Any color preferences? And so forth.

CHAPTER 7

It's all about the pauses: why parents need
to give multiples time apart

One of the big preoccupations of parents of multiples is to what extent their children should be given time apart. Decisions must be made about it, and those decisions fill some parents with unnecessary dread. Yet, this should be straight-forward: it's about getting a chance to be your very own person, not always be what your sibling is not, and getting your own stories that you can tell in their entirety.

To be honest, I was surprised to learn that some parents are hesitant to give their multiples time apart, thinking it might break the twin connection.[97,98] As one worried triplet mother put it in an online forum: *Who am I to break the connection they've had since the womb?*

Reading that, my mind stirred into instant alertness. I suddenly became aware that my take on this ran contrary to current thinking among many parents. It surprised me, because of all the dilemmas you face as a parent of multiples, I admittedly thought this was one of the breeziest to maneuver.

Certainly, for multiples, or any child, the chance to pee in private, tell a story in its entirety, and even miss one's siblings just a little help strengthen the bond in the long term.

Let's also remind ourselves what we learnt in a previous chapter: multiples have a primary attachment to each other. All children need to eventually separate from their parents to become complete, little people. We multiples have this process a few times over. Some time apart from one's co-multiples simply means getting a head-start at finding out who you are and realizing that you are capable of being on your own.

While some parents refer to time apart for their children as "separation", I suggest we start calling it for what it is, "a little pause". To realize why that is so, we need to be clear on our starting point, and I am not exaggerating when I say that it's extreme. Researchers point to how multiples' social experiences in this world are distinctly different even from children who have siblings close in age.[99] We go about this world with a double identity: an individual identity and a couple identity (that would be "the twin" or "the triplet").[100,101] And the reason why? We share a social world when little. That's the conclusion of an Australian study on twins and friendships, which showed that twins in their early years rarely have a chance to be in a social setting without their co-twin.

Now, at a superficial level, sharing a social world of course sounds rather lovely. My overriding memory of early childhood is having someone to play with. Ask young twins or triplets and chances are, they'll be quick to point out the same. Ask parents of multiples and chances are, they say it's certainly well deserved. While the feeling of being outnumbered is likely to linger, parents quickly realize that the math also adds up in their favor: Inbuilt playmates.

It's like a friend with twins said: "The best thing about having twins is seeing them play with each other, having a total blast." That idea is that of the "extraordinary friendship of twins," as one researcher calls it,[102] and is why what I'm telling you now might seem counterintuitive. Because if your multiples have a blast together and there are lots of other children coming around to your home, then why should you intervene to make sure your children also get experiences apart?

It becomes apparent if we rather describe the shared social world with this finding by American psychologist and renowned twin expert Joan A. Friedman, also an identical twin and mother of fraternal twins: "Twins lack privacy because they're born into a situation where they are within their twinship nearly all the time."[103] Friedman's among the twin experts in this world that's prepared to argue until the cows come home for twins' choices.

Why is it, she asked at a world congress for twin experts, that the same parenting issues that have confronted families of twins for the last fifty years are still ever present? The expert diet for healthy twins, she argues, is as straightforward as it has been for years. Here's her snap recap: "Help others distinguish between them, treat them as individuals, encourage them to do some things differently and some the same, encourage them to do what they need to do to separate from each other, and teach them to relate to others individually."[104]

Alas, efforts to help twins become individuals remain stultified. In an article titled 'Scrooge of Twinhood', Friedman says she at times feels like a lonely crusader in a culture obsessed with twins and that is idealizing the twin bond: "I do not regard the challenges twins face as abnormal; rather, I am taking the challenges out from under the shadows of twin mysticism and helping twins embrace selfhood." Mind you, when I read this, my crush on her grew. Yet, as I snuggled up in the sofa with her book *Emotionally Healthy Twins: A New Philosophy for Parenting Two Unique Children,* I couldn't get past the obviously worrying image of Friedman as a lonely miser in a world of twin unicorns and stardust. While we'll skip an intervention by three ghosts and leave the 'twin mystique' back in chapter five, here's a three-part list from a fellow Scrooge to get more people's heads convincingly around why multiples should get some time apart from each other.

1. Let's call a spade for a spade: it *is* a little pause

Now, the intensity of a life as a triplet is hard to convey to singletons (and even twins), so let's start this on an Indonesian island with a story that might be more relatable. After six months of backpacking together with my then-boyfriend, now husband, I had a go at him one evening, angry and on the verge of tears, for finishing my stories. *I can't do this again* had been running through my mind half the evening, and when it was finally just the two of us alone, swatting mosquitos inside the low-budget hut we'd rented, I let it all out: "I can't do it. I can't do it again. You can't take my stories."

I pretty much just blurted it out, leaving my boyfriend— bless his heart—wondering what in the world had gotten into me. We'd just spent a lovely evening with some fellow back-packers, and suddenly I was breaking down in front of him.

But why?

More and more on our travels, the two of us had started to nudge in a detail here and there when the other spoke—the small but crucial detail needed to properly tell the story. Or, at other times, one of us would digress entirely, injecting a proper backstory that would be of help to the listeners. We both knew very well how each story went: we had both been there, and we were both excited to share. But that night, he took it up a notch. As he took over *my story* entirely, he also awoke long-forgotten memories of not always owning my stories because someone else—both my sisters—had also experienced the same and could correct me if I'd gotten something wrong or if they were eager to finish the story before I did.

So, when I said, "I can't do this again," I was thirty but also speaking on behalf of my eight-year-old self.

Most adults can imagine that turning an already close relationship into a 24/7 happening may at times feel like too much, but this is nothing compared to the sharing that goes on in the lives of multiples. If this is how two adults ended up talking on top of each other after only a few months of continuous companionship, how is it then for children who continuously share?

Here is a random day in our household between the age of six and sixteen:

- In the morning, I meet my sisters in the upstairs bathroom. With seven people in the house, one bathroom has been assigned to just my sisters and me. (If I came to a locked door, I'd check if it was a sister or brother on the other side; while I would let my brothers pee in peace, if a sister replied from behind that locked door, I'd bang until she let me in, because, obviously, if a sister was just having a pee, I could come in and use the sink or the mirror.)

- We sit next to each other in the kitchen for breakfast, and we return upstairs together to brush our teeth.

- Leaving for school, my sisters are next to me in the entryway, where we put on identical jackets and bicker about whose shoes are whose, as they are all new, obviously identical, and haven't yet been labelled—yet one pair has a bit of mud on them, though no one claims responsibility.

- My sisters are next to me as I walk to school with backpacks identical to mine, there again when I raise my hand to answer questions in class—their arms held just as high as mine—trying to get the attention of the same teacher.

- At recess we play together with the same children.

- At the end of the day they walk with me home, sit next to me in the kitchen while doing the same homework I am doing.

- They are with me when we run out to play, next to me when I watch TV or when I start telling Mum about my day—because it has also been *their* day—and they rush in to tell part of the story before I tell it all and correct the parts they think I've gotten wrong about what had *actually* happened.

- They sit next to me at dinnertime and come with me when I head out for football practice. After we bike home together on identical bikes, we eat supper together before it is time to call it a shared night and once more brush our teeth alongside each other, are jointly read to by a parent, and go to bed at the same time.

My sister Trude says it is a closeness that is impossible for any adult who's not a multiple to relate to. "What if we still lived in the same apartment, had the same neighbors, sat with the same colleagues for lunch, reported to the same boss, and outside work we had the exact same social group. If people can imagine how artificial a situation like that is as an adult, then maybe people can relate to what it's like to be little and must share and compete about everything.

"Imagine, if you're at a team meeting at work and then your boss turns to you and your two other colleagues who are also your sisters, and she asks, 'How are you guys getting on with the task?' and then everyone answers on top of each other... Or she only asks one and doesn't bother to ask the others because she knows you're doing the same anyway."

2. Are your multiples speaking fast and on top of each other? It is wholly understandable.

I once read a comment by a doctor who's authored parenting books on twins, saying, "twins excel at interrupting. Many of them need to be taught to speak at an appropriate pace."[105]

That's not it, I thought when I read that.

Don't put this squarely on twins. Rather, teach the rest of the world to treat us as individuals.

One of the clichés of twin and triplet connectedness is that we finish each other sentences. But triplet ducklings Huey, Dewey, and Louie in Donald Duck speaking fast and on top of each other is not an illustration of deep understanding: it's a matter of little children eager to tell their version of a seemingly shared story before a sibling beats them to it. It's not cute. It's annoying as hell and it's not their fault. They're simply working within the framework they've been given.

As little, "How was your day?" truly was a pointless question if not asked separately. It wasn't a question at all: it was the starter pistol commencing a verbal race. If I waited, I ran the chance of having a sister spoil my story or leaving me with nothing to tell. Thus, our parents would often divide up stories in three parts, with each question addressed to one: "How was your day, Mariann?" "Now it's Trude's time to tell." And: "Now I would like to hear from Kari." This made it possible for me to (hopefully) get to tell my chunk in peace and quiet.

Yet, there were shared experiences where there was effectively no incentive to wait for one's turn, such as one episode after the summer break when we were about eight or nine. At school on the first day back, our teacher asked everyone to share what they'd done during their vacation.

Almost everyone, that is. The teacher skipped one. 'We'll pass Trude now and go directly to the next. We've heard now from both Mariann and Kari, so we know what you did during your summer holidays."

Trude was crushed. "It's sitting in a classroom," she says, "hearing you tell the story, then Mariann, and thinking there's nothing left to tell, and then hearing the teacher say the same thing, that now we will skip Trude. That he didn't get that it wasn't about a detailed run-through of events, it was getting a chance to share. And add to that the fact that we simply accepted it as children. Children are all about fairness, and I'm sure we would have protested strongly if the teacher had said that we'll now skip Kjetil because Karen was also in Legoland this summer and she's already told everyone what that was like. But when it came to us, we accepted it. Why didn't we protest?"

It's a telling episode of how it's easy to lump multiples together, even by adults who are trained professionals and should know better than treating multiples as a single unit.

3. Learning to be on your own and relying on yourself is a major part of life's curriculum

Of course, divvying up stories as a parent and asking your twins or triplets to answer individually by using their names will only take you so far. You need to up the game by letting them get a chance to ace this world on their own, without an ever-present side-kick or two.

Back to Joan A. Friedman, as this is her field of expertise. Speaking of the magic of individual experiences for twins, Friedman says: "If you give them experiences where they learn to be on their own, where they learn to rely on themselves, they develop a resilience, so they can feel they can be their own persons. If not, then they develop this overdependence, or really a co-dependence, because they've never been without each other."[106]

I wasn't all that surprised to learn that this dependence might be stronger for twins than triplets. After years of studying twins, Swedish researcher Britta Alin-Åkerman followed seventeen sets of triplets in Sweden from birth until they were nine years old. The triplets always played with each other, and if two in a set fell out, there was always the third. Alin-Åkerman refers to how many of the trios expressed a strong dependence on each other, but this, she believes, was not as strong as in twins. Perhaps, she says, due to the numbers at hand: "Twins only have each other while triunity gives more choices."[107]

I get that. As Trude once told me, "You are so close to me that I may criticize you, but no one else is allowed, because then they indirectly criticize myself, right?"

But our sister Mariann is allowed.

Over the years, I've had someone else I could turn to if I was upset with one sister: my other sister. It makes me think that triplets have it easier than twins.

But, the belief that multiples are best kept together is a stubborn one. Parents might also be stumped to realize that it's their very own children that are hesitant to the idea of a pause from one another, and if you ask them, they might find it plainly unnecessary. And, when you eventually go ahead with some pauses anyways, they might find it downright uncomfortable, confusing and even painful.

Because just like for parents, it's reassuring for a child to be sent off together with siblings into unknown territory, whether it's kindergarten, school, a bus journey or the first sleepover, as there *is* strength in numbers. Being with one's co-multiples gives a child a certain boost in their self-confidence, and most of the time it's wonderful to be together.

Mariann agrees, saying, "Like when we were ten and Mum brought us along for a weekend at a hotel where she was to attend a conference. While she attended meetings, we played in the hotel pool, with only a few breaks now and then for 'a triple-portion of French fries, please,' a quick visit to the reception for some of their free candy, and yep, putting on some evening shows. We entertained the entire political group in the evening with songs and jokes and walked around in identical tracksuits. People staying at the hotel smiled to us and knew our names. You get much more attention as three than as just one little girl out and about."

Yet, the reason I chose this example is because it's less obvious that you should do something in this situation than when you face the stereotypical twin red flags, like the dominant twin who does the talking and the silent follower, or the introvert duo or trio who don't want to socialize with anyone else.

But even in a group of three extroverts, there might be someone eager to be the alpha. You don't want one to assume a more dominant role, thereby forcing the other(s) to take on a more subordinate role. One way of dealing with that is to give them separate experiences—a few pauses.

Of these dynamics when we were little, Mariann says, "I spoke a bit with Trude about it. Trude said she felt you could be a bit dominating. I replied it was worse for me because I felt that both of you could be dominating. And Trude was incredibly pleased, she could not stop laughing. She thought it was brilliant that she was also dominant. You were often the one who was pulled out at home. I remember Mum once said that you had tried to become the leader, and that we had put a stop to that. But I do remember that we pushed you ahead of us, every time someone had to do something, then you had to do it, and Trude and I were pretty pleased with that."

"Like the lambs?" I ask.

"Yeah, those kinds of things," Mariann replies with a laugh. "Kari will fix it!"

The sheep at a nearby farm had recently birthed lots of lambs, and the three of us headed over to ask if we could see them. On the way over, I told my sisters they also had to talk. Yeah, yeah, they promised. *Of course they would.* I remember they were seemingly offended I asked, but still, not overly convinced, I demanded we all stood alongside each other, facing that slightly scary front door to the house where those strangers lived.

Just as feared, as soon as I rang the doorbell and just before the door opened, the two little traitors took a step back, leaving one in front—the one who had to do all the talking.

Who knows; maybe I sought to take that role because I was continuously told I was the oldest. "We're the same age," we'd reply when people asked—or, more honestly, that's what I said if my sisters were around. If the question came when I was on my own, I spared the person the inevitable follow-up question, the one where they pressed, "Yeah, but who was born first?" and I'd go straight to the good part with, "I'm the oldest. By two *and* four minutes!"

Our parents tried to downplay those minutes. "It doesn't matter. You were conceived at the same time and you were in the stomach and alive at the same time."

They were wrong, however. Those minutes mattered immensely to everyone we met.

They still do. Because unfailingly, the world really wants to know. It likes to have us all figured out. Multiples may seem like a small hiccup to the system of assigning personality traits by birth order, but my answer of "two and four minutes" have always put the question to rest and brought welcome clarity to the ones listening. I am the oldest.

At a recent party, a man in his late thirties introduced himself, said he knew Trude from before and asked me who was the oldest. But when I replied that we were triplets, assuming he wanted to know who had a year or more on the others, that wasn't it. He was after the minutes.

"Oh, I know you're triplets," he hooted. "So, who's the oldest?"

"By those four minutes?" I asked cheerfully, in a tone I hoped said, "surely that's a really silly question to ask?"

"It's you, right?"

There. That's how the world is wired.

I'm the oldest.

As a parent, you might be wondering whether you should indeed tell your children who was born first. I say yes on the basis that it's a stubborn fact: your children will be asked about their birth order, again and again and again. Failing to answer something perceived as the bread and butter of who we are will undoubtedly drum up a whole new line of questioning, now centering on why in the world your parents wouldn't give up this valuable nugget of personal information? Your coping tactics instead come down to tackling the issue head-on, by being aware of the stereotypes of birth order and steering clear of self-fulfilling prophecies. (For more on this, flip back to chapter four).

Yet, Mariann isn't sure. "For us," she said, "I think it was more important to know who weighed the most." And then we both laughed.

CHAPTER 8

Why every day shouldn't be a sibling playdate and how to help twins maneuver friendships

In which I dwell on the uniqueness of twins' friendships and how sibling relationships of multiples are the odd-ones out. The cliché of in-built playmates means parents may rob multiples of a much-prized sibling-privilege: closing the door on one another. I address how twins share friends, and while often wonderful for the friends, the pressure to always include each other is challenging for multiples. And here's this chapter's spoiler: Maneuvering friendships for twins is mainly about edging towards what friendships are like for everyone else.

After you've given birth at Oslo University Hospital, you're supposed to head down to the cafeteria to receive visitors. Thankfully, the perception of the close bond between multiples works in our favor this time—twice.

"They said no at first," Trude says, standing in the middle of my hospital room, holding a handful of flowers, a small box with a bracelet for me, and a card welcoming my son. I don't quite follow, so she connects the dots.

"I'm not supposed to be here. 'But I'm her identical triplet sister,' I told them. And their reaction? 'Eh, ok...' So they let me go up, *ha ha ha.*"

Two hours later, Mariann politely pulls the same line, and whether it was the same person or not on call, the midwife, puzzled, lets her in. At times there are benefits in being *potayto, potahto.*

Yet, here's an inarguable, scientific fact: for most children, the feeling of being *potayto, potahto* isn't always enjoyable. Here is a story from my childhood that makes my father chuckle every time he tells it. In fact, he finds it so hilarious he included it in his speech at my wedding.

One day the doorbell rang. My father opened it to find a little boy standing there.

"Can I play with the triplet?" he asked.

"Which one?" my father replied.

"Doesn't matter. It's all the same to me," the boy replied with a smile and shrug.

My father laughed as he let the boy in, saying he'd find the girls upstairs.

I get that it didn't matter. The child's main concern was gaining entry to the house with the "play room" with a climbing rope and a ladder hanging from the ceiling, a pink trampoline surrounded by cushions, and boxes upon boxes with toys, dress-up clothes, and books, not to mention the feeling of "the more, the merrier" as more and more children rang the doorbell to join in on the fun.

Yet, truth be told, I don't like the story my father tells.

"But why?" my husband wanted to know, adding, "It's hilarious!"

That may be so, but for me it brings up feelings of being *potayto, potahto*. I knew all too well that other children could just as well play with my sisters as they could with me, and that many had no idea which triplet I was.

Friendships are different for twins

These days, I've looked up the research, but I was already spot on as a child. Multiples don't go about choosing friends in a vacuum—potential friends obviously respond to us. We tend to choose friends who are like ourselves. Among multiples the ones of us who share interests and look similar, and indeed those who are difficult to tell apart, are likely to have the greatest problems in making friends independent of our co-multiples within the same social pool.[108] This means that when we make friends, we establish friendship alongside our same-age sibling(s). Australian researchers Karen Thorpe and Karen Gardner point out, that the twins might see each other as competitors for friendships or might operate as a unit. With years under their belts of socializing with one or more children of the same age, twins might bring to the table better negotiation or cooperation skills. Yet, the flip-side is the chances of a too-close relationship between the multiples that impedes the development of other friendships. We'll deal with all of this, but let's first have a look at what researchers call the most notable feature of twins' experience: twins *share* friends.[109]

Twins share friends, especially if they are identical twins

The fact that multiples share friends is not surprising. Friends tend to come with geography when you're little. Also, if twins are normally kept together, be it in kindergarten, school or in extracurricular activities, their pool of potential friends remain the same. A British study that surveyed 11,000 twins at the start of their schooling found that only eight percent had their own circle of friends; the majority had shared friends, while twenty percent stayed together and had few other friends.[110]

But what's important to be aware of is that friendship patterns appear to differ with what type of twin you are: identical, same-sex or opposite-sex fraternal.[111] An Australian study of thirty sets of twins found that identicals shared half of their friends, fraternal same-sexed shared one quarter, and opposite-sex pairs only meagre five percent. The twins also had different takes on what it was like to share friends:

- Boy-girl twins didn't report any issues. Frankly, not a surprise. Sharing is not all that hard if you have 95 percent of your friends to yourself, and any shared friends with your co-twin belongs to a larger social group and is not either twins' perceived best friend.
- Opinions by fraternals of the same-sex differed the most. Some were ambivalent or negative about being a twin and sharing friendship.
- Identicals were reported to be "positive or accepting" about shared friends.[112]

When you look at these figures, parents of identicals might wrongly assume that their children are all breezy about sharing friends. Yet, based on my own personal experiences, whether you're "positive or accepting" are different ballgames.

A shared social world also due to strong social expectations

While "play nicely together now" is a common parenting phrase, twins and triplets hear it more often than other children. Parents need to be aware of the strong social setting on top of the genetic situation, especially for identical multiples. We simply face stronger expectations towards being together and including each other than what regular siblings and even fraternals do.

Researchers point to an assimilation effect for identical twins and a contrast effect for fraternal twins: the physical similarity of identical twins and the stereotypical ideas of twins lead people to view and treat us as a unit, expect the same of us and confuse us for each other. We also tend to have more similar experiences than fraternal twins, spend more time together, and are more likely than fraternal twins to influence each other in the direction of conformity.[113,114] Parents of fraternal twins, however, are more likely to search for contrasts between their children, highlighting differences in physical characteristics, personality traits and abilities, and more prone to let their twins go their own ways.

My point is all proven when I ask my father how we played together as little. He says, "We did have a rule that all three had to be able to join in, so there was little exclusion going on over time. You were together most of the time."

At first glance, good rules; two weren't allowed to exclude one. If one had a friend over, all had to be allowed in on the game. No one was to be left out. Also, that friend coming over might be everyone's friend or classmate or on everyone's soccer team, and you want all your children to have a good time, to not compete over friendships, and not send other children the message that some of your children can be excluded, at least not in their own home.

Unfortunately, that's not what life is like for regular siblings. You might inadvertently be robbing your multiples of a much-prized sibling privilege: closing the door on one another.

As a child, I always thought my brother Stig, two years older, had it easier. He had us sisters but got to be entirely on his own as well. Stig could play nicely with us for a while, but at one point decide enough was enough, take his friend, and leave. "Kjetil, come!" he'd say. "We're going up to my room!" And the two of them would head upstairs to my brother's room, locking the door on the world and the siblings outside.

The downside of a shared friend? It's *everyone's* friendship

The Australian study on friendship should have added an additional classification in the research type: *type* of shared friends. There are the ones you meet and make at the same time, and the ones you meet, make friends with, and *then* need to share with your siblings. One of the identical twins in the study, who did not like sharing, did indeed point this out:

Researcher: How do you feel about sharing your friends with your twin?

Lachlan: Mmmm it's like if they are candy, it is like they're candy and I have to give most of them to my brother...

Researcher: I wondered whether sometimes you fancied having a friend that you didn't share with your brother? Or perhaps you haven't had any opportunity to have separate friends.

Lachlan: Well sometimes Nicholas... I usually spend all the hard work getting friends and Nicholas steals them off me.[115]

"I completely get that, and I of course agree," Trude says. "Sharing friends you've met on your own is more annoying than sharing friends everyone met at the same time. I remember when I made friends at the cabin and then it was a bit like, "Oh no, I had to introduce them to you two and then you again had to compete to be the one the friend liked the best."

But even in a situation where all would go on to play together, it's not all plain vanilla-sailing. Not only do you need to share a friend you might have preferred all to yourself, but you also see the thread of your friendship reflected in the behavior of your co-twin(s).

I'll let Trude explain: "There is an expectation that everyone should play together, and you should share everything all the time. And, when you meet a friend, they don't only have to like you, they need to like everyone, because everyone is to join in. That's why it becomes incredibly important how your siblings behave.

"But, you don't always want to share. Sometimes, you want to have a friend to yourself. At the same time, you don't want to close that door and behave badly towards your sister. So what Stig could do because he was two years older, we couldn't, because we were in the same class and our friends were our classmates."

As my sister points to, one of the problems with demanding that everyone plays nicely together is that it presupposes that whoever comes over to play is a friend of both twins or all the triplets. If you must play with all of them to get to play with one, then it's crucial that you like all three. The snag is obvious. For a multiple, the power balance to your friendship then suddenly rests with your co-twins. And, it is of course not unthinkable that a friend doesn't necessarily want to play with both or all three.

And, bear in mind, this is also about relieving your children from the burden it is to be accountable for someone else's happiness. Your multiples might be tremendously loyal. It took Trude 25 years and reading this draft chapter before she admitted, "You know my friend whom I played with at the cabin? The reason why I mostly went to hers instead of playing with her at our cabin was that she didn't like you and Mariann that much. She preferred just being with me. I never told you that. I didn't want to hurt you."

What when sharing a friend is breezy – how is it for the friend?

My sisters and I had a shared best friend when we were little. Henriette, the girl next door, one year older, twenty centimeters shorter and a daily playmate since our mothers plonked us down together in the sandpit outside our houses.

Although four makes an excellent combo for most games—like Batman and her three Robins—at times it's really tempting to have a friend all to yourself. Sometimes I'd nip over to the neighbors' house, but just before I'd ring the doorbell I'd peek in the window. Often, I'd discover that a triplet sister had beaten me to it. Just like me, but only minutes before, she'd quietly put on her shoes and slipped out of the house without a word. (In truth, with two sisters out of the house it normally didn't take long for the third to do the math and head on over too.)

What about the shared friend though? What's it like to be the close friend of a group of siblings?

"Really cool!", Henriette says cheerfully, when I call her up for some reminiscing.

"Our lawns overlapped, so we almost became half-siblings. Or, if you think of how close we were for a period, it was almost like sisters," she said. "I went by yours almost every day. I'd go over and ring the doorbell, and then we'd play wherever it suited best, whether at yours or at mine, all of us or just with one you. Sometimes you'd invite others as well, and then there would be even more children playing."

So what were the positives about being a friend of triplets?

"I always had someone to play with. Normally at least one of you were home. Also, we were able to play different kind of games than if I'd only played with one other child and we more easily came up with new things to do. It was genius. You didn't have to run around half the village to gather enough children to do something because we were already four."

And the negatives?

"There were of course disagreements now and then, but we were so close that we could say what we meant. We might argue, but then two hours passed, and we were best friends again. Sometimes the three of you would fight between yourselves though. Then I thought, "Who am I supposed to choose to be with?" Because I almost felt like I betrayed the two others if I only played with one, because I didn't have any favorites. There were none that stood out as, "You're the one I play the best with".

"Although you looked similar, you were of course entirely different people. Mariann was a bit more the quiet one, Trude the one who was a bit sillier and more jokey, and you were a bit in between. I had a great time with all of you, so there was never an issue of "Oh, I don't want to play with that one." I adjusted very much to whomever I played with as well."

Sometimes though, we really wanted to have Henriette to ourselves, just one-on-one. A challenge with shared friends is the occasional attempts to upstage your siblings, to be the one that's more fun, the preferred one, the one that gets the most attention from that exciting non-sibling. I tell Henriette this, and ask her if she recalls what it was like to be the coveted friend.

"I never felt uncomfortable or anything. It was more on the contrary. I remember that Trude came over during Christmas once. She had glued three nuts together, which she was going to give to Cinderella, and then of course I was Cinderella. [This is from a scene in a Czech film that is shown on Norwegian TV every Christmas, in which the soon-to-be princess is given three magic nuts, each providing her with a wish] I kept those for ages. You wrote a beautiful letter in calligraphy for my birthday once that you came over with. It was cool actually."

My first thought when Henriette mentioned Trude's gift? *I don't remember that; maybe Trude gave them to her in secret?* That was part of it: we did compete for her attention. Sometimes we passed her gifts in secret so that the others wouldn't know and upstage you.

Speaking with Henriette, I tell her about a friend of twins who said she thought it was hard when those around always looked at the twins as one, whereas she knew how different they were.

"Well," Henriette says, "when others talked about you, it was always about "the triplets." It was never Trude, Kari, and Mariann. I then tried to differentiate you, but that of course never worked. Mum never managed to tell you apart—"It's one of the triplets"—and that's how it was everywhere. "It was one of the triplets." "So, which one?" I always asked. No, she wasn't sure about that. I felt that no matter what, you were always seen as one."

This leaves me slightly baffled, so I need to double-check.

"By your mother or others?" I ask.

"In general. You were always seen as one."

It's not that I'm surprised, but I'm somewhat surprised at my own reaction. I feel sad. It's something about having your own idea of things so brutally confirmed by someone else. Because up until then, I could have been mistaken.

But no.

"Even though I always said Kari, Trude, Mariann, everyone else said "the triplets." There were many times I felt like there were talks about "it was one of the triplets," even though it might have been just one who had done something bad or stood out positively. "Yes, it was the triplets." "Okay, so which one?" I asked. "Yes, one of them."

"What was it like for you then?" I ask her, "Who was so close with us and so easily told us apart?"

Henriette says she ended up taking things with a pinch of salt. "I thought that if they didn't manage to combine the who and the what, then it wasn't easy for me to take a stand. Because I knew how different you were. Sometimes I could guess which one they talked about, but it wasn't always easy. So, if it was about something negative, I just thought, "Okay, but if you can't tell me which one it was, then don't bother saying anything at all then." I often ended up just pushing it a bit at a distance. Because I couldn't go in and defend you either when they said, "the triplets." That was one of the disad-vantages of there being three of you."

So, what do you do then as a parent?

1. Can't face those shut doors? Then let them go else-where.

If it pains you to see one of your children exclude her siblings, the solution is simple: let them do it out of sight. That was normally on offer for individual friends, like with the best friend I had at the start of primary school. "If you want to be with your friend on your own, then you can go to her place." That's probably why I normally went to hers; if I brought her home I had to share her. At her house I had her to myself. I didn't have to compete for my friend's attention.

2. Let them more easily play with quieter children.

While some shared friends soak up the attention, multi-ples may come on too strongly for some children. It's not necessarily easy to be on the receiving end of two or three people's undivided attention. There were those who got overwhelmed at the level of activity and ener-gy. "Yes, but it was a bit much." That's a quote from a girl who came over for a play date once. A one-sentence sum-up when asked whether the day at ours had been fun. After that, Trude went to the girl's place for play dates on her own.

3. Make a shared friend all theirs from time to time.

Shared friends can also present opportunities for indi-vidual friendship experiences. Change sharing to turn-taking. I recall the sleepovers at Henriette's, both the many that the three of us joined in on but even more so the ones I went on my own. One by one, we'd stay at hers. Often though, Henriette and the one who spent the night would still play with the two others during the day, but come dinner and night time, she was all yours. I'm sure the triplet rotation also worked well for Henriette's parents; having just one additional child staying overnight or joining for a trip may feel like a different ballgame than the prospects of bringing along two, let alone three additional children.

4. Let others approach them as one person, not one group.

As a parent, it's up to you to show other parents that your children can spend time apart. Just like many parents of multiples, the parents of your children's friends may think that multiples are best kept together. The likely downside of that is that the number of playdates or excursions might dwindle to nil, either due to practicalities like space in the car, expectations that their singleton might feel left out or worse yet, get ganged-up on, or for not wanting to hurt the feelings of the twin that doesn't get to join.

Your job as a parent then is to start issuing single invitations and open a space for other parents to reciprocate.

5. Help your children bear not always being included.

A few bruises here and there is part of life. It might be painful to not be included, but the world is not always even-handed. You can however do your bit in levelling things: if not all your multiples have playdates at the same time, it might be an opportunity for you to do something one-on one with the child remaining at home. Rather than feeling left out, they get a parent's undivided attention for the afternoon. Or, let them get the choice of inviting a friend over to your place.

To sum-up, supporting friendships for multiples is about expanding your children's choices by letting them at times be on their own, enable others to approach them as just one, and letting them focus on, well, themselves. Because when you send your children on individual playdates, when they get to have a friend all to themselves—to not have those others always there—you're sending a message that it's okay for them to focus on what they feel, need, and want, and that they don't have to feel guilty or bad for not always including or being there for their siblings.

And, here's the key bit: whether your children truly are each other's best friend, now or down the line, well, that's something they must be allowed to discover on their own. Giving them a sense that it's okay *not* to choose each other from time to time may make it easier for them to choose each other down the line—and it might make it possible for them to hold onto some friends that are just theirs.

CHAPTER 9

Being samebody: the pros and cons of having body doubles

Life is full of contradictions, and the one that dominates mine is the perception of my body as identical to my sisters' but finding myself surprised whenever I see similarities in our faces. This is the piece on the pros and cons of having body doubles.

When Mariann recently uploaded a new profile picture, Facebook immediately sent me a push notification. "Mariann Ertresvaag added a profile picture you might be in."

I clicked my way to "photo review" where a large "call to action" button stood below the photo of (just) Mariann, telling me to "Tag Yourself." Facebook boasted how it found the photo using face recognition technology. I didn't tag myself, but I shared a screenshot with amused friends and a group for parents of multiples.

"My gals have also demonstrated the limitations of Apple's face recognition. They can open each other's phones," a mother of identical triplets tells me.

"Our Nest doorbell camera can't tell my three boys apart either. #identicaltripletproblems," another chimes in.

"I was wondering how this works for identicals," a third says.

"It clearly doesn't," I reply.

One of my colleagues offers a thumb up, saying, "If I can be mistaken, then Facebook can as well!"

Yet, the differences are there. For starters, I have two four-millimeter scars.

The scar, the mole and the nothing

It's hard to imagine today as we've grown to look increasingly different (spoiler: epigenetics. See next chapter for the full explanation), but when we were little, a minuscule mole resembling a freckle and two scars were the tiny differences that helped people tell us apart.

"I'm Kari. I have scars. See!"

If I'd met you as a six-year-old, that's what I would have told you as I pointed next to a spot beside my left eye. There are two scars, although most people spoke and still speak of it as singular. "The scar."

Yet, if you knew me, I wouldn't say anything. I'd stand there quite still while you crouched down to have a look, hoping you'd get it right, that you'd finally go, "Ah, the scar, now this is Kari then."

If you'd met me today, you wouldn't see them; you'd assume it was a wrinkle. I'm also certain I wouldn't point them out. Much in the same way Trude wouldn't let you know about her mole—the minuscule dot she has on the tip of her nose—and Mariann wouldn't tell you that she has, well, nothing.

On the one hand, the fact that a mole and two scars were used to tell my sisters and I apart says something about how similar we looked as children. On the other, it sums up, more than anything, what I seek to convey with this book: life as an identical multiple is often life under a magnifying glass. Any mark, no matter how tiny, becomes that needed element of differentiation both for others to tell you apart and for you to set yourself apart. What would normally go unnoticed becomes important. Like a mole.

Our body, yet *my* face
That facial recognition comes up short for multiples, is difficult information for all twins and triplets. It was—and still is—our faces that were used to identify who we are. Over the years, when people have failed to tell us apart, excuses have invariably revolved around not having seen our faces properly. "Oh, I only saw you from the side," people say, or, "I didn't see your face; I saw you from the back," or even, "I didn't see your face properly." Our faces are simply in a different category than the rest of our body, as with most people. A "selfie" is of our face, not our elbow.

Also, there's simply no arguing that my body is not also the body of my sisters. It's a conversation I'm not overly proud of. But really, you would have done the same thing if you were in my shoes. I have a humongous gap between my big toe and the next toe. I didn't notice it myself. My helpful husband did: "That's so weird. There's a massive space there. It's like someone amputated a toe of yours!"

Afterward, it was all I could see. I had to brief the sisters, because if your very own clones also have a toe gap, it's not weird. Really, it's nothing to be concerned about.

Almost nothing.

"I thought *nothing* about it for twenty-something years," Trude says, "until one day we were sitting out on Dad's balcony and you guys pointed it out—something about how we had good preconditions to become these kind of feet painters. And then—*then*—then I saw it: a gaping hole. There was room for another toe! I found it funny, but also bizarre that someone else could make me aware of something about my own body, after all, in one I've lived in for many years, that I hadn't noticed. I think you were both there and I asked you not to tell me anything else that was wrong with my body. It's bizarre. Here you have two people who know your body just as well as you do and sometimes better, because it's their body too."

Being an identical multiple is not only about having someone who looks like you but about having someone on the same page as you throughout your entire life. It's like the photo a mother of identical triplets shared on Facebook: three girls grinning next to each other with her caption: *"We lost our first tooth!!" said Addie!!! It was out of Emma's mouth!! Lol."*

Just like these little girls have realized, what's at hand is a set of bodies that pretty much delivers in the same way. Which might be why the magnifying glass is still very much present also when we look at our bodies. It explains why multiples can pay lots of attention to half a centimeter difference in height. Yes, as with all children, the cool thing was being tall, but I would add that it's not just about being taller. That half a centimeter makes you different; it's what's not the same, it's what's just *yours*.

"At one point during our teens," Trude says, "our heights were measured. You were 178 cm, Mariann 178.5, and I was 177.5 cm. I was always a bit frustrated with that. But at the age of 35, I was part of the control group in a medical research project and they measured my height to 178.8 cm. Absolutely fantastic! I was so thrilled I had the doctor write it down on a piece of paper. It wasn't about the actual centimeters but that I was taller than you. I wasn't the shortest one. I enjoyed thinking about that for days. What rational 35-year-old would normally be over the moon for being 0.3 and 0.8 centimeters taller than her siblings?"

When I ask my sisters how they see our physical similarities and differences, Trude says, "I have no difficulties saying that my body is your body. Our bodies are almost identical. The way the bodies are shaped, everything from nails to toes to the size of our teeth. When we say we're very different, we focus on our faces. There are differences—we used them ourselves when we were little to help people tell us apart, and then others used it too. But even the differences in our face are small variations, like Mariann has a slightly different nose, my face is a bit rounder, right, there aren't any big things distinguishing us. We are a bit more similar than we normally admit."

(True, even I was surprised when I discovered I could use Trude's dental mold to bleach my teeth, made for her by a dentist by casting plaster on her teeth. And if you're wondering, the reason why I used it is simple: vanity. If we are to be standing next to each other, we'd want to measure up, and neither Mariann nor I were eager to smile with cream-colored teeth next to those pearly-whites. Mariann, however, had to get her own mold, since she sucked her thumb as a child more.)

(Similar) appearance also involves choices

Mariann, however, takes it further, giving me a run-through of what ought to be obvious: appearance involves choices. "I think our differences in appearance is more down to the way we dress, use make-up and what we place emphasis on, so how that affects the way we look."

She reminds me of the coasters my father once received for Christmas, with photos of the family over the years.

"Dad thought one of me was actually you. I had borrowed clothes from you, you helped put on my make-up and you did my hair—in the same way you would have done if it was you, so then I of course looked like you. Another time Trude did my makeup and hair and afterwards she jokingly said, '*Aaah, mini me!*' So, if we wanted to look similar, then I think we could have been very similar. But, I would like to be me, you would like to be you, and Trude would like to be herself. And therefore we also look more different."

It's also what happened the day Facebook had us utterly confused.

Mariann had called me that morning, asking for photos of me so that she could show the hairdresser what kind of highlights she also wanted. Afterward she texted me a photo, saying, "I look like you!"

Facebook agreed.

Thankfully, we all live happily with our contradictions

Yet, every now and then, I flick through one of my sisters' photo albums and I'm struck by the similarity also in our faces.

I say struck, because whenever I see it, I find myself surprised. "I look like Mariann here!" I once said out loud in surprise, whereupon my husband replied with trademark British dryness, "There's a reason for that."

I realize that my father has similar thoughts when I call him to ask about a recent holiday he's been on with my sisters. I tell him how I had been taken back by how similar in appearance Mariann was to me in one of their holiday photos. "Funny that," he replies. "I sometimes accidentally said the wrong name to Trude and Mariann while we were there. But there was this one time when I called Trude for Kari, and you know, she just looked at me a bit surprised. I then took the time to look a bit more, and I was surprised to see how much you two really look alike."

I understand my father's surprise because I find myself surprised at times as well. Our overall appearance is pretty much identical and there is no denying the same body shape, but that acceptance falls under the provision that our faces are solely our own. Our faces have always helped people set us apart: moles, scars, and everything. Thus, we find ourselves surprised, like our friends and family who look at us and say it's not hard at all to tell us apart—but who then suddenly find themselves taken back when they scrutinize a face and see the similarities they normally downplay.

That's life in general—the facts don't always fit. Life is made up of contradictions and most of the time we happily live with them. If they're our own. Like my face.

Pros and cons of body-doubles

There are some obvious downsides to identity confusion, but having lookalikes in this world comes with some pros and cons. Here are five stories that sum it up.

Pro 1: Body-doubles can make life easier.

It's within the capacity of your very own clones to make you feel entirely normal. At no point were Trude and Mariann more welcome in my life than during puberty, when most teenagers struggle to understand the concept of normal, let alone how to fit into it. My sisters were my medical dictionary, the instant kind I could ask everything that I thought our mother wouldn't be able to answer or that I simply wasn't keen on asking anyone else. And if they didn't know, we would brainstorm.

"Do you think they'll get any bigger?"

We were about twelve, in Mariann's bed for a heart-to-heart while looking from one flat chest to the next to the next. I recall speaking with great expectations of what was to come.

When I ask Mariann about the benefits of this seemingly shared body, she recalls the same episode. "Developing breasts," she says, "is something girls would normally find themselves going through alone. One day you realize you have this hard lump and you're left to figure it out on your own. But in our case, it was a matter of, let's say, brushing accidentally into one of your sisters and being sternly told off because hers were a bit sore. It was the idea that you could sit down and compare and talk so intimately with someone about these kinds of changes."

Pro 2: Extra cake and hugs.

"She went down there *again!*" my mother would say with a chuckle whenever she told us this story. One day she looked out the kitchen window and saw one of her girls chatting with the neighbor out front; the neighbor handed her daughter a piece of cake and the girl slipped around the corner of our house. It didn't take long before the same girl appeared. Again she rang the neighbor's doorbell, again she was given a piece of cake, and again she slipped around the house, out of sight. I'm not sure what my mother was thinking the third time she watched the same girl receive a piece of cake from the neighbors, but I'm pretty sure one little person was superbly happy with being a multiple.

Not long ago, I was walking down the street in Oslo when I heard someone shouting, "Mariann. Mariann. *Mariaaaaaann!*" I took me another few *Marianns* before I realized this was probably directed at me. I stopped and turned around and before I had time to react, there it was: a hug. The guy introduced me to the woman he was with.

"This is Mariann. We used to work together."

"No, actually, I'm the sister," I replied.

"Oh yeah, they're twins. Trude, right!" He turned to the woman he was with. "Yeah, I've met them both before."

"No, Kari," I replied. "We're triplets. I'm not Trude or Mariann."

The girl, by now fully amused, took in what I said, but the guy was busy explaining the twin thing to her. "They're twins, and I used to work with Mariann."

"No," I insisted, both the woman and I now laughing. "There're three of us!" I held up three fingers. "We're triplets. I'm not Mariann nor Trude. I'm Kari."

"*Whaaaat?*" He laughed. "That's insane!"

"It happens," I said. "It's not a big deal."

I got a big hug again as he left.

Pro 3: Escaping socially awkward or boring conversations.

Okay, I'm not overly proud of all these instances, but you know when twins and triplets snub people? It might not be our siblings, it might be us. I was out jogging one day when 200 meters ahead I saw the familiar face of someone more acquaintance than friend but still someone it would have been natural to stop and speak with—but I was in a bad mood. I was cold, and I just wanted to get home. That's when I remembered: he knows that I'm a triplet. So when he scrutinized me for any signs of recognition, I told myself I was one of my sisters, one who wouldn't look in his direction. Yes, I jogged straight past him.

Con 1: Losing acquaintances.

Over the years, multiple people have obviously been mistaken. The confusion is only an issue, though, if people think it's just, well, *you*. Of course, this might be related to willingly passing ourselves off as a sibling, but it's also scientifically proven (probably) that having an identical multiple will lose you acquaintances—like the girl in the bathroom at the University of Oslo one day when I was twenty. I recall smiling at her but not getting a response. She took many of the same classes as me, so I found it quite odd that she merely returned a flat look.

But, as I was about to leave, she spoke up. "Do you have a sister that goes to this faculty?"

"Yes," I replied. "Two."

"Are you, like, triplets or something?"

I nodded, finding it odd that she asked. I would often hang out with Trude and Mariann while at campus, but we rarely told people we were triplets and, as far as I knew, this girl didn't know them.

"Thank god!" she exclaimed. "One day you would pass me, give me a big smile and say hi. The next you'd walk straight past me." She laughed a bit, seemingly embarrassed at this point. "I had actually decided never to say hi to you before you said it to me, as you seemed either crazy or very moody."

Oh God. I was still "the triplet"?

I hurried up those stairs to tell my sisters to start smiling at any happy stranger in sight, wondering how many people on that campus found me to be rude beyond belief.

Con 2: Going down for someone else's crime.

Can identical multiples get away with crime? We discussed this as children. If we each gave each other alibi and left no fingerprints behind, that would surely be the perfect crime? There wouldn't be any "prisoner's dilemma" because we wouldn't tell on each other. There would be reasonable doubt and we would all go scot-free.

It's not such a far-fetched scenario. Identical twins have gotten away with drug trafficking,[116] plane theft, and even murder.[117] Each occasion included a mix of bewildered eye witnesses who couldn't distinguish between the two and an unwillingness by the twins to rat out a sibling.

While we were right on much regarding getting away with crime, we were not always right on the scot-free bit. Once, at the age of eighteen, I puked outside a nightclub. It happened at a social event where most of our friends had been. Except me. I was never there. Despite Trude's repeated pleas to join, Mariann and I had decided to stay at home that evening. Trude went on her own. When Trude turned up to school the following Monday, mortified at how the day would turn out as she had been sick outside a club, she was served a wholly welcome question.

"I heard your sister Kari was really drunk on Saturday."

Thinking quickly, she replied a noble, "Uh-huh."

Well played, Trude, well played.

Chapter 10

Identical multiples are clones, yet allowed to differ

In which I explain that I am a clone, though a unique, faulty one. You see, no two or three people are *completely* identical, not even us identical multiples. Definitely reassuring, but the challenge becomes apparent when identicals or our parents again and again need to explain to people why we're deviating, and increasingly so with age, from the agreed mold. So—here are two explanations of epigenetics for when you're in the line of questioning: one with all the science-y bits intact, and one that explains this through chocolate cakes. And, as a bonus for not so similar looking identicals or fraternals, here is also an explanation of the phenomenon of context.

A week ago, Trude called me. "I think you would like to write this down."

She'd left my new apartment just minutes before, so I was a bit confused. She'd run into my neighbors on her way out, she said, and it turns out they were confused as well.

"I met a woman who went 'Hey Kari!' as soon as she saw me."

"Oh, that must have been Emma," I replied.

"She didn't say her name. Anyway, I said I wasn't you but your sister, okay? And then we came out onto the street. 'Hey Kari!' That was her husband. 'Oh, I'm not,' I said again, and they started apologizing. '*Soooo* sorry. Sorry, sorry, sorry.' I said it wasn't a big deal, that it happened all the time. 'We're triplets,' I said, 'identical.' And then the woman cocked her head a bit, looked at me and went, 'Not identical-identical.' *Ha ha ha*, put that in your book!"

True indeed. We're not *identical-identical*. No two or three people are *completely* identical. In a futile attempt to make that clear, some researchers insist on calling identical multiples "monozygotic" and fraternals "dizygotic." But I'm here to burst their bubble, it doesn't help. In my native Norwegian, "monozygotic" is literally translated "one-egged" and we still face expectations of being *identical*.

Do a poll, identical multiples are expected to be *identical*

If you're nature's copy and paste (and paste), you should be like the coffee table books that display the most identical of the identical crop, with faces neatly sliced in half and put together as one. Two halves of what could have remained one. Few people know identicals personally, but they've seen the films, yet not stayed for the credits that say one actor played both twins.

Because obviously, any identical twins depicted on TV have to be properly identical. We are clones after all. During summer of 2005, when we were 23 years old, my sisters and I watched *The Island* at the cinema. Clad in clingy white jumpsuits, Ewan McGregor and Scarlett Johansson (a fraternal twin in real life) live in a sterile facility with other clones, whiling away their time in ignorance until the day they're due to be harvested for spare parts. A bucket of popcorn later, it turns out that clones have souls. There's even enough free will around to let the two eventually escape and track down the humans that had them cloned as handy spares. In the end, McGregor and Johansson sail off in a boat together, and we left the cinema with wide grins. This wasn't just a dull sci-fi movie; this was to some extent reality. If I need a kidney, I know whom to ask (or harvest).

I always knew I was a clone. But I knew it as a *joke*. In the same way my colleague did, when he pointed to the new printer room at work, bearing the sign "clone tank."

"Check it out. It's an office for you and your sisters."

The definition of a clone is bafflingly lacking

But researching this book, I learned the very definition of a clone. It comes with no difficult biology words, no affixes derived from Latin or Greek, no long-winded, complex sentences. In fact, it's so mundane, so totally boring, so missing of anything proper science-y (nil!) that it seems like a bunch of biologists were about to nod off at the meeting where it was discussed. "Fine, a clone is a clone," someone eventually summed up, "let's just say 'naturally occurring' or 'artificial', ok?"

Done. Sorted. Lunch time!

This is it, ladies and gentlemen: "Clones are organisms that are exact genetic copies. Every single bit of their DNA is identical. Clones can happen naturally—identical twins are just one of many examples. Or they can be made in the lab."[118]

Answer courtesy of the renowned Genetic Science Learning Center at the University of Utah.

Now, why does a definition matter? It matters because when you run a Google search on "cloning explained for kids," this is what the Internet answers:

- 'You might not believe it, but there are human clones among us right now. They weren't made in a lab, though: they're identical twins, created naturally.'[119]
- 'Although they are genetically different from their parents, identical twins are naturally occurring clones of each other.'[120]
- 'She [Dolly] is actually a carbon copy of her mother, like an identical twin.[121]

I used to think that people used the phrase without knowing what it meant, that when I brushed off other children's comments about how I was a clone, they were in the wrong. But as it turns out, I was. When it comes to the definition, Dolly and I are two of the same. Personally, as a newfound clone, I would have preferred a giraffe to have been cloned first, or a seahorse, or any other animal that doesn't lend itself so easily to the cliché of mindless clones. But no, first came a whole bunch of sheep.

The definition we have misses the essential bit: no one's a copy

The tabloid version of the artificial method, called *somatic cell nuclear transfer*, is two cells from different sheep, an egg cell without its nucleus and DNA and a cell from an udder with the gene-bearing nucleus intact, a tiny jolt of electricity through the two, bada bing, bada boom, and they fuse to an embryo.[122] That's also how we're entirely different, notwithstanding that one is human and the other a sheep, and surely someone can head back into a meeting room and dish up a better definition?

Dolly was a clone of a six-year old sheep. I am a clone of two others that were created at the very same moment as me. It was never a matter of an original and a copy, or a first, second and third edition. It's a matter of not having to answer "so, who's the copy?" Though on a side note, an identical twin I know managed to get the nickname 'The Draft' ("Kladden" in Danish) stick on his brother. Both brothers and their friends happily still use it, well into their thirties. I'm sure all second-born twins would tip their hat to him.

To pass on genes, only *one* pregnancy is needed

As children we thought the benefits of our shared genetics would be substantial. With our basic knowledge of DNA and genetic inheritance, surely *one* pregnancy would be enough if we were to pass on these genes? Why should everyone have to go through labor? We discussed it mostly as a joke, but the nugget of truth in our theory had Mariann very upset when both Trude and I pointed to her: she had to do it.

Joke or not between multiples, researchers put it black on white (they thankfully also put in a few double quotation marks, but it still makes for bizarre reading): "When identical twins marry and raise families, each twin becomes a "genetic parent" to their nephews and nieces (their twin's children). These nieces and nephews become their aunts and uncles' "genetic" sons and daughters. This happens because identical twins are clones, making them biologically "interchangeable."[123] Our children, then, aren't first cousins, but, and here I quote, "genetic half-siblings" as the "two sets of children have the 'same' mother or 'same' father."[124] Genetically speaking, I'm equally related to my sisters' children as to my own. (Don't tell my nieces and nephews, as they may then hand aunty Kari completely unreasonable Christmas wish-lists).

All clones differ—both artificial ones and naturally occurring ones. Why?

I've wondered about this myself and you might be wondering as well. Why do we look different if we have the same DNA? Why have we become increasingly physically different with time? Because ask me today and I won't have difficulties pointing at myself in a recent photo. But, there are numerous childhood photos of me that both my sisters stubbornly insist are of them. (Our father overheard us one day we were discussing who was who. "You don't know?," he asked surprised. At the time they had thought of that, he said, so we were positioned in birth order in most photos. That didn't really settle it though, except for Mariann in the middle. Because, did the positioning go from left or right?)

As a child, we either looked too much alike or too little. On the one hand, I had the ones who would zoom in on similarities, who would repeatedly tell me that we looked the same, who'd confuse me with the two others. And then there were those who would make it into a game of spot the difference, and who'd in the end wonder out loud if we really were identical because they could tell us apart. Take it from me, nothing is more absurd than having to argue the point, while you're trying to overcome the hurdle of similarities and being mistaken for your sisters, that you are indeed identical.

The fact largely missing from most people's biology lessons is that the environment comes in and muddles things. So let's add some knowledge here. Because when I looked into this, I felt relieved. And the reason I felt relieved is of course the element of doubt that's always been lurking whenever someone quizzed us on our appearance. Were we deviating too much? Were we not doing a proper job at being identical? Were we not actually identical? Could the doctors have gotten this all wrong?

Thankfully, I now know that I have the environment and the knotty world of epigenetics on my side. I get to be entirely unique while also identical. Because my neighbor was right: I'm not identical-identical. And, that ladies and gentlemen, is due to more than genes, namely epigenetics.

Explanation of epigenetics No. 1: The one with all the science-y bits intact

The DNA sequence of identical multiples' genes are the same[125], but there's more in the pudding. There are two chapters in our body's instruction manual[126].

1. First part: DNA, genes and genome.

Think of Russian Matryoshka dolls in diminishing sizes placed inside each other. The smallest doll would be the DNA, which is the molecule that carries genetic information and is the smallest building block there is. For humans, 99.9% of our DNA is the same. For most humans, 0.1% is then the bit of DNA that's different from anyone else's. In actual numbers, that amounts to 1.4 million differences[127]. But, if you're an identical multiple, it's zero, nil, nada. Not *one* of those 1.4 million differences that the rest of you have all to yourself. Our DNA match is an even 100 percent. Every cell in an identical multiple's body has the same underlying genetic code as the cells in his or her co-twin's. And like everyone else's DNA, that genetic code is fixed for life. So, genes are made up of DNA. And our so-called genome is the entire Matryoshka doll, our complete set of genes, about 21,000 or so per person.[128]

2. Second part: The epigenome – what makes each of us unique.
Now, let's move on to the *epi*genome. For identical multiples, this is the crucial bit. It's what makes everyone unique, even if we're clones. While our DNA can't change, and our genome is with us for life, the *expression* of those genes can change. Genes interact with the environment and can be turned on or off.[129]

There's a bit of Greek going on here, but it's rather helpful. The prefix "epi" means "above" or "beyond" genetics. There are millions of chemical tags on our DNA and on the proteins that sit on the DNA. This second layer is the epigenome, which tells the cells what genes to express or keep silent. The epigenome responds to signals from the environment to activate or silence different genes, although the underlying genetic code remains unchanged.[130]

The reason identical multiples become increasingly different as we age is that we receive an increasingly amount of different input. Our environment, and thus also our epigenome, is fairly similar at birth and through our early years, and then it becomes increasingly different.[131] For the start of our lives, my sisters and I ate the same food in fairly similar quantities, we did the same level of physical exercise, we had a shared bed time, we went to the same school, and experienced similar life events. But then our environments started to differ more, and we started to accumulate an increasing amount of individual epigenetic modifications.[132]

We have the genes we have. Yet, stress and nutrition, but also exposure to toxins, like smoking, differences in physical activity, in sum all our lifestyle choices and whatever life throws at us can affect biology. Scientists are diving into this as we speak, trying to figure out how the environment can change the behavior of our genes. A Spanish study that looked at 40 twins between the ages of three and 74 found a progressive development toward more difference.[133] In brief: Different lifestyles, different outcomes.

Like one of my positively unhelpful colleagues pointed out one morning many years ago as I walked into the office where I worked.

"I was just in Budapest," she said, a woman in her fifties, "and I met your younger sister at a meeting."

"Oh cool," I replied enthusiastically. "We're the same age though. We're triplets."

"Huh," she replied. There was a pause. Admittedly, I waited for her to smooth things over. But, things weren't boding well. She looked me up and down. Complete body scan. I hardly had time to think, *Wow, that's rude,* before she said, "It must be stress and nutrition then."

She gave me a quick smile and hurried down the corridor to her office. I changed direction from my desk to the coffee machine. I deserved to start the day with a break, thinking, *I shouldn't stress, it affects the looks.*

Explanation of epigenetics No. 2: The one with the chocolate cakes

Say "epigenome" to an eight-year-old or even your average 37-year old, and their eyes gloss over. That's why we also need a child-friendly explanation.

Thankfully there are researchers out there like Anne Matthews, Professor of Genetics and Genome Sciences, who explain epigenetics with imagery like baking chocolate cakes.

I first came upon Matthews in an article explaining grandparents if their grandchildren would look like them. Genes aren't the sole ingredient in the 'oven'—or the woman's womb, she explained. There are also lots of non-genetic environmental factors that can potentially have a major effect on a fetus.[134]

As with every time you bake a cake, Matthews pointed out, "even if you think you put in exactly the same measure of ingredients and cooked it at the exact same temperature as before, it never comes out exactly the same way. The shape of a nose alone, for instance, has to do with hundreds of genes all working in concert."[135]

I decided to contact Matthews and ask for more. Could she by any chance also explain why identical multiples end up looking increasingly different? Preferably with the help of some chocolate cakes too?

She could indeed:

"You are correct—the concept of epigenetics is not an easy one for anyone to explain! I guess if I was to use the chocolate cake analogy to explain differences in identical twins, triplets, etc.—you might say—one batter of chocolate cake was mixed but then split into three different pans. It is often difficult to pour exactly the same amount in each pan so that might make

a difference. If you put them in the oven—each will be sitting in a different place—the temperature might be slightly hotter in one area of the oven so that cake might be slightly different from the other two pans. Did the baker move one or two of the pans around some but not the other—might lead to how the batter is distributed in each pan.

"While identical twins are born with identical DNA—the expression of their genes may be slightly different from one another because of environmental factors—the mother's diet, stress, exposures during pregnancy—although all three babies are exposed, the exposure might not be exactly the same or in the same amount. After birth—while the DNA does not change—epigenetic changes, which are biochemical changes, are ongoing—so twins and triplets may look a bit more differ-ent from one another as they grow older."[136]

There you go, courtesy of a unique, faulty clone. Forget Dolly the sheep when you are to explain this to your kids, go for Matryoshka dolls or variations of a chocolate cake!

Our brains take shortcuts, and that's why many find it hard to tell multiples apart

Why do people confuse us? I'm going to take a stab at this and say that all identical multiples ask this question, and 50% of all fraternal twins do as well; those other 50% are boy-girl twins. (The gender chances of a fraternal twin pregnancy are; 25% chance that a mother will have two boys, 25% chance that a mother will have two girls, and 50% chance that a mother will have a boy and a girl.) According to researchers, it's partly due to people's inclination to view twins as a natural unit and partly down to our brains taking shortcuts.

To help others tell us apart, similar looking multiples are quick to point to a slightly different nose, a scar, or any other differences that make us stand out. But, as I discovered as a child, that often requires a rather close examination of all three at the same time. While multiples might feel confident that people can finally tell us apart once we've pointed out our small differences, our brains don't work like that: it turns out that brains don't recognize faces feature by feature; we don't store faces in our memories as collections of noses and eyes and so on. Instead we remember the whole face. If you see someone in a crowd that you think looks like your friend, well, that was your brain shuffling through its archives until it came to a good (enough) match.

I learnt all of this on The Open University website in a series of blog posts by Graham Pike, a Professor of Forensic Cognition. Pike's research is mostly on eyewitness identification and facial perception. His scientific contribution tends to be in the realm of police investigations, but I figured he might also be the right man to explain the conundrum of twin confusion.

I contacted Pike, explaining how people confuse my sisters and I, although we no longer look as similar. I asked him whether it's a matter of seeing what you expect to see, or does the way we remember faces play into this? Since we look so much alike, are the differences in our faces picked up on if they just see one at a time?

"What an interesting issue!" Pike replied, and what he wrote next made all the pieces of the puzzle come together. A lot has been written about context, he said, and it is a very powerful phenomenon. So interesting in fact, that I'll share everything he wrote:

Essentially, our minds take cues from a particular situation to let us know what to expect, and also who to expect. For example, if you regularly go to the same supermarket you might begin to recognise some of the staff there, but would be very unlikely indeed to be able to recognise them if you saw them in a different context, such as walking down the street. Even with more familiar faces context can have a large effect, such that seeing someone you know in a new and unexpected context (bumping into a work colleague on holiday for example) can lead to you having difficulty recognising them—often having a sense of familiarity but not being certain where you know the person from. Once someone becomes very familiar (good friend, family member etc.) you will be able to recognise them despite changes in context of course, but having siblings that look like you would mean that context would again become important. If someone who knows you, sees one of your sisters in a context where they would normally expect to see you, or indeed an ambiguous context, they may well mistakenly think it is you. In other words, although we like to think of our minds containing definitive information that is always "correct," in reality we are heavily dependent on a number of shortcuts (such as relying on context), which makes us prone to making mistakes in unusual situations.[137]

It was indeed an unusual situation both for Mariann and her new colleagues the day all fifty of them managed to ignore her.

In our late twenties, my sisters and I ended up in the same line of work for about a year. We lived in different countries, but we were all somehow connected to the Norwegian Ministry of Foreign Affairs—so connected in fact that a lawyer in my office forbade me from touching anything relating to Hungary to avoid any conflicts of interest. While I was at the European Free Trade Association in Brussels, Trude was at the Norwegian Embassy in Budapest, and Mariann had just started working at the very section at the ministry back in Oslo my unit was reporting to.

As was the custom, Mariann and one of the other new colleagues flew down from Oslo to Brussels to meet their new "colleagues."

"I flew down from Oslo to Brussels," Mariann says, "with another new person to say hi to everyone. But your colleagues thought *you* gave the new person a tour. No one bothered to pay me any attention, so I had to stretch out my hand to everyone. They simply thought it was you showing around the new person. I remember telling you off afterwards, saying 'I really think you could have informed people that I came down!'"

CHAPTER 11

When your in-built buddies don't count:
why adolescence might be tougher for twins

Adolescence is uphill for most, but for a multiple there's more potential for, and here I quote a twin researcher, "the giant wave that overwhelms everyone."[138] While you're trying to define yourself outside your twinship, the world regularly bursts in to compare, contrast and reapply the label of twin or triplet to your back. While this piece deals mostly with the beast of bullied multiples, there's also comfort in here that parents should pass on to any teen multiple.

Before we properly start, I need to put preteen and teen years for multiples in perspective. Like everyone else, multiples search for answers as to who we are, any answers really, that can give a little firm ground to stand on. But on top, we need to develop autonomy from our co-twins.[139]

The challenge is how to do so when so many stubbornly perceive you as the same as or compare you with just one or two others. You're still not seen just as you; you're first and foremost part of a group, "one of the twins" or "one of the triplets."

In a US study of nearly sixty adult twins, the interviewed twins said they rebelled against being compared with each other as teenagers. According to twin expert and psychologist Barbara Klein, who authored the study, teenage twins became angry with continuously being compared and started pulling away from their twin, trying to define themselves as unique persons.[140] As teenagers, they tried to take up separate interests, friends and clothing to establish a separate identity outside of being a twin.[141]

Some reassurance for parents fearful of their children being bullied

The most comprehensive study to date on twin-singleton differences and bullying found neither a higher nor lower risk for twins, whether as a bully or a victim.[142] This Dutch-British study, which included close to 10,000 Dutch twins aged 7, 9–10, and 12 years and their non-twin siblings (as a control group), found no effect either based on the genders of the twin pairs or the twin's zygosity, so whether identical or fraternal. The study authors did however find that girl–girl twins were bullied less often when placed in the same classroom.[143]

There's also an interesting case study of seventeen sets of triplets in Sweden, followed from birth until they were nine years old. Of the triplets studied, seven sets were fraternal, nine trios were made up of two identicals and one fraternal, and one was all identical. Study author Britta Alin-Åkerman notes how the triplets were extremely popular and had no difficulties making friends. The triplets were never bullied or excluded by any other group of children, and if one got into trouble, the others rushed to the rescue. Alin-Åkerman writes, "They were completely loyal and supportive to each other on such occasions, which means that together triplets form a very strong team, and no one dares to tease them or be unkind to them—a common occurrence among children of this age."[144]

Nonetheless, I need to raise the shoulders of parents of multiples a tad.

Because as I read these research findings, I wondered what the outcome would have been if the twins and triplets in the studies had been followed past age nine or twelve years.

I ask because while my sisters and I gathered all thirty children from our two parallel classes for a celebration of our tenth birthday, we celebrated our thirteenth birthday with just the three of us, along with Mum and Dad at a pizza restaurant.

Bullied as a duo or a trio: What is it like and how is it even possible?

I wasn't going to share at first, thinking it wasn't a story of everytwin or everytriplet, but then I read a story by a triplet mother on an online parenting forum. *No one wants to sit next to my triplets during lunch break*, she wrote. They were frozen out, they had no friends, and no one spoke to them. I took to Google, typed in "twin bullying" and found many who would have happily outsourced their preteen and early teen years.

In a thread on the twin forum a boy wrote, *As an identical twin, I felt like I got more than the normal kid's share of bullying when I was in middle school. Anyone else out there with similar experiences?* he asked.[145]

That's when I figured I should tell my story.

And as I read the online comments left by lonely twins, I realized that while all stories are unique, a list of commonalities was forming in my head. We'll run through these as well as my own story with the help of some of the comments I found (in italics below).

1. Your children stand out

From the twin forum: We were ostracized a lot because of being twins in primary school. But in high school, there were lots of twins, so it wasn't a big thing.

A psychologist once said that everyone can become a prime target for bullying. The challenge for most multiples, and even more so for identicals, is that you stand out from the crowd. That's not necessarily a good thing when you're eleven and your main goal in life is to blend seamlessly into a group.

So what happened to us?

Our mother asked Trude this very question once. "What happened? You were so popular?" The two-part question stung, my sister says. I can, nonetheless, understand why our mother asked. In our early childhood years, we would have fit right into Alin-Åkerman's study of extremely popular triplets until the age of nine.

"I knew the answer to Mum's question," Trude says. "We got grades. But when *she* asked those questions it really hurt. I then felt like it was my fault that no one wanted to be with me."

We were clever, which ranks high on the bullying roster, and we flaunted it (see next chapter). Trude dryly adds, "It probably didn't help that we all had braces, glasses, and '80s perm-curls."

Indeed, there we were; three glasses-wearing, rail-thin, flat-chested, brainy girls, each wearing a poodle on our heads. This made me think of a conversation with an American girl my sisters and I met in our twenties, who said, "Thank god you're good looking! There's nothing worse than ugly twins—because there's two of them!" (Let's clarify with this quote from our brother Stig about our early teen years: "You were never ugly—you just had hideous accessories.")

As an adult it's easier to look gently upon children. When I tell a friend how we were bullied when we were eleven and twelve she asks, "What do you mean? Bullied how?"

I give her a quick recap to our social leprosy: being perpetually ignored, not included in activities, and best kept at a distance. It's hard to imagine today that if my lunch box wasn't in my backpack, I'd actually go and look for it in the bins in the toilet or in the classroom, that someone could open the door to the toilet with scissors from the outside while I was in there, and that if I sat down next to someone they'd pull their desk a centimeter away from mine.

"Yet, in fairness," I tell her, "I do see that we were annoying to a lot of the other children." I shoot my arm up in the air, wave it around and make her laugh. "Imagine three of these at every, and I mean *every* question that ever arises in *any* class, while you sit there still trying to figure out the answer to what the teacher just asked."

The catch is that while I was a star in the classroom, as soon as the recess bell rang, I descended to the very bottom of the social hierarchy.

2. Your children already have someone in their corner—each other—so others can skip it and keep their heads high

From a twin forum: There were plenty of times I rushed to my sister's defense in school. Nothing made me angrier than people trying to upset her and vice versa.

"Your jackets are outside."

It happened repeatedly for two years, and that was all that was said by the girls that sometimes would come and let us know. I still recall the burning sense of shame and embarrassment as I rushed to retrieve the jackets, hoping that the ground wasn't wet, that the jackets hadn't been put inside-out and that there wasn't anyone outside to witness the indignity of retrieval, not a wall of five, ten, or twenty other children watching in silence as I (or all three of us) picked up the jackets without a word before hurrying inside to put them back on the pegs so we could pretend it hadn't happened.

My sisters and I never spoke about it as children, and we never once asked any of the other children if they knew who did it; it didn't feel like it mattered. No one protested, no one ever picked up the jackets, no one ever flat-out told us who did it.

Children normally have well-developed moral compasses, but they could sit this one out. As a child I never understood why none of the girls who would tell us about the fate of the jackets couldn't simply pick them up, but as an adult I get it. To do so would be to tamper with their own fate in the school yard. Also, this wasn't a matter of a timid, little person on her own, but three girls who all seemed strong enough in class. And, if you were to rush to their defense, what would be in it for you? Preteen years are a time of intense one-on-one friend-ships between girls, and our trio would have been a formidable one to break into. Becoming friends with one sister wasn't really an option; it would involve all three.

That said, I'm fairly certain that if you'd ask any of the other children back then, they weren't bullies. The traditional victim of bullying is *one* person. This wasn't a matter of a group against one, it was *group* against *group*.

Trude says, "I think it's a situation where others would normally have reacted. But if it's three, then it's okay, you don't have to act, it's the quiet majority that's watching. Maybe if it was just one jacket, then someone might have reacted and said, 'we can't keep doing this.' But you're taking three... the problem was that that group felt a bit like one person... we were one unit. I didn't feel like that they were picking on me, Kari and Mariann, it was on *us*, and they probably thought we had each other."

3. Your children can't just be themselves because they're also each other

From a twin forum: It didn't matter how different me and my twin where they treated us the same. I was more outgoing trying to make friends etc, but her negative attitude and such they figured I was the same.

Also: They called my sister the evil twin and shit like that, they'd also make fun and say oh you've got a fatter face, you're prettier to try play us off against each other.

Being seen as interchangeable serves up some psychological hardship. If you're constantly confused for someone else or perceived as being just the same or having a group identity that's more clearly out there than your own as an individual, then you can't just be *you*. You have two others policing you—because you're also *them*.

"The triplet" was someone three girls wreaked havoc on. Whenever any of us did something deemed wrong by the two others, we'd all become tight-lipped. You'd look at your sister in shame and horror at what she had just done. What *you* would soon have done. When people talk about how their spouse embarrasses them, they've got *nothing* on what it's like with siblings that people see as *you*.

Trude says, "It was obvious why we didn't like being called 'the triplet.' Then it wasn't a person any longer. It was a group, a group no one liked, one that did too well at school."

She pauses, then continues: "I had a feeling that no matter what I did, I had two others that reflected on me. I often felt that the criticism didn't go toward me, that it was something Mariann or you had done or said. I remember once after gym class, some of the girls in our class told me they liked me best. I remember thinking, *why couldn't you just tell me that you liked me?* Because saying they liked me best put the two of you down, and also it wasn't much of a compliment to be told they liked me best within a group few people liked very much."

4. Siblings don't count as friends

From the twin forum: Sometimes we would not be invited to things and the reason was 'we could only invite 1 more person and we couldn't just exclude one of you.' Well I think that may have actually just been an excuse but anyway… Also when our class were told to get into pairs we would sometimes be forced to go together (even though we didn't want to). But I think that was just because neither of us would have someone who wanted to pair with us. No one seems to understand that after being twins we are sisters! No one else would willingly hang out with their sibling. Fuck I hated primary school!

Parents of multiples might find this tricky to understand. Surely multiples have each other and they get on fairly well together at home, right? While you might consider your children to be best friends, they look at each other as siblings. And, blood relatives, twin or not, do not count in adolescence. What counts is belonging to a group of friends or peers, getting that feeling of being accepted, the very thing psychologists say is at the core of teens' self-esteem.

According to Trude, "In the sixth grade when we went to camp with our classmates, I didn't want to share a room with you and Mariann. I desperately wanted to share a room with someone else, because I really wanted to show that I had friends. I felt that you two were more okay with being in a group together. But as far as I was concerned, it was almost worse to be in a group with you. That felt like such a visible proof that none of us managed. That no one wanted to be with the triplets. Maybe that was why it was so important for me to be in a different group than you, so I could show people that we could be with others, we had choices. It was embarrassing if we all were in the same group."

Unknowingly to the other two at the time, we each thought, *If it had been just me, would it have been different?*

Mariann says, "It was very much a split issue. On the one hand, you were my best friends. I remember we walked together around the school at recess, and that felt very good. But at the same time, it was a bit negative because it meant I had no one else. It was the three of us for better and worse. I felt that it was not because I was me that I was bullied, but because we were three."

You might think it's easier to be excluded as a trio than if this happened to just one child, that it would enable you to deduce that if this also happens to your siblings, vastly different from yourself (at least in your mind), then surely, it's not really *you*.

Unfortunately, that's how adults' reason but not children.

At times, paradoxically, it felt worse that my sisters knew what happened at school: it meant there was no escape. My sisters had also been witnesses to the events. It had also happened to them. And, they came home with me every day. It couldn't be made to disappear, it wasn't possible to deny, and I couldn't pretend it didn't happen. Perhaps that's why we never spoke about it.

I assumed they thought and felt the same as I did around this. In hindsight, I was correct about that. I was wrong, however, about how they didn't count. Most siblings grumble at each other in their teens, but then grow up and realize the gold that's been there all the time, just next to them. Trude captures this well when I ask what she would tell herself if she could go back in time.

"Enjoy your sisters. Hurry and join them for group work. Regard them as your friends. Don't forget that they're yours. Why do you care about the others? If I get a visit by you and Lillian now, then I get a visit by two friends, and of the two you're worth a bit more. If I had felt that also as a child, I would have had two best friends through middle school."

None of us can go back in time, but what I can do is tell a whole lot of parents out there what my sisters and I would have appreciated hearing. Obviously, my sister's comments won't be persuasive to an eleven-year old. But what you can do as a parent is to share this chapter with any preteen or teenager in your household, as there is a sliver of comfort in knowing that while this time of your life is really hard, others have thought so as well, and it gets better. As a comedian, once a bullied child, said of what she calls her awful school filled with horrible people, "you'll be free one day. They're not allowed to keep you there."[146]

So, tell them that one day whom they get to hang out with won't be limited to the ones in their classroom or their village. They will have the world at their feet, and when that day comes, they get to choose whom to hang out with. Chances are, they might even choose their siblings. At least sometimes. Not because they have to, but because they want to, as they really are some of the coolest ones around.

CHAPTER 12

Competition in the triplet lab: why multiples should get their own class at school

Admittedly, I'm biased on this one. I will bluntly tell you to opt for different classes for your children. Parents do their best to avoid having children compared or measured against each other, but if you put siblings together in the same class, it is inevitable.

A team of external consultants recently assessed the management teams where I work, including mine. They conducted personality tests, put us through case interviews in one-by-one sessions in which they also had us describe in depth as best as we could who we were as persons—the whole shebang.

After a marathon-length interview of me, I met one of the experts in the cafeteria.

"I must admit," I said, laughing, "I left that meeting now thinking *'What in the world did I just tell them? Everything?!'*"

"Yeah." He chuckled. "That's why we do four hours, nonstop. No one can keep it up for that long."

When he returns a month later to give me the results of the assessment, he tells me I am very self-aware.

"It comes from being an identical triplet," I reply.

When I look up the research on this, my DYI psychoanalysis is spot on.

When nearly sixty American adult twins were interviewed by psychologist Barbara Klein, an expert on identity development in twins, they all believed that part of their identity or personality was related to the fact that they were continually measured against each other while growing up.

Klein notes, "Twins internalized the comparisons others made between them and always compared themselves with each other. This focus on what was similar about their experiences and what was different made them very aware, almost self-conscious, of the choices they made. In many situations' twins' identities, either as a pair or as an individual, was overdetermined because of the amount of attention it received."[147]

That's the crux of the multiples' world. The quest for differentiation means that even minor things, the kind normally deemed irrelevant or which go unnoticed, can become a distinguishing feature. What is the same gets overlooked, while what is different is worth noting. The scar, the mole and the nothing.

Putting siblings in the same class is systematized comparisons

"Just do your best." It's one of those messages you're flooded with as a child. But what if your best is also someone else's best, that just next you, in the next swim lane, at the desk opposite you, or on a higher branch of the tree you're climbing, there's a reminder that your best could be that little bit better? And what if there are two of them?

Parents do their best to avoid having children compared or measured against each other, but if you put siblings together in the same class, that is inevitable. Comparisons are more likely (for friends, teachers, and yourself) if you have a measuring stick or two sitting next to you. It's also how our school systems are set up, and that's what grades do—a score is written down and you're compared with other children.

School placement is perhaps the biggest headache for parents of multiples. Unfortunately, there's little research to help you out, though opinions are plentiful. That's what American psychology professor Heather Beauchamp found when she reviewed the available studies on twins and education.[148] And, unsatisfyingly, the few studies that exist largely look to parents' and teachers' perceptions on the benefits of keeping twins together or apart, rather than twins' own perceptions or their psychological and behavioral outcomes.[149,150]

Parents in favor of having a say in the matter (usually to keep them together) point out many good reasons. It's simply more practical, some say, having one set of homework to help with, one school excursion to plan around, or a smaller group of other parents to get to know, rather than close to a hundred. Many believe it would pose unnecessary anxiety for children to be separated, and some believe it might hinder them from getting the famed twin bond.

Parents who separate their children do so in the belief that it's healthy for them to experience the world outside their twinship, and for a myriad other reasons I'd be quick to back them up on.

The New York Times article on school placement and twins, which first introduced me to Beauchamp, nonetheless mentions two later studies that came after her review. These studies, one Dutch and one British-American, found that "twins separated early were observed to be more anxious and emotionally distressed than those who remained in the same class." One of the studies, which included close to 900 pairs of twins from ages five to seven, found that this was especially true for identical twins.[151] Parents should be aware of this but also bear in mind that many twins have limited experiences in being apart when they start school, and a separation in different classes then may be challenging.

That said, given that the number of long-term studies on this are effectively nil, I'd like to offer a take on why it nonetheless might be challenging to keep the children in the same class.

A physical separation to find yourself

My sisters and I were in the same class all throughout primary school. We grew up in a rural community tucked in next to a Norwegian fjord. Of the 700 people around, twelve were in our class; seventeen were in the parallel class. My parents discussed it at length when we were young, that it was unfortunate we didn't live in a larger place so that we could have been placed in separate classes.

With only two classes available at our grade, my parents pondered questions like: Who should be placed in the class where the pupils lived geographically close to us? Who should be put together and who should be on their own? And, how would a split in two and one impact the bond between the three?

While I'd say it's best to put multiples in different classes whenever possible, I'm thankful they didn't go for just two classes for us three. However, it did mean a rather intense competition between the three of us.

When I read twin expert and psychologist Joan A. Friedman's take on school placement for identical twins, I therefore felt relieved, because it's nice when someone pats you on the back and says, "It *is* hard. You were right in finding it difficult." Not only is Friedman a proponent of different classes, she says that in some cases parents might even want to consider different schools for their identical twins around the time of middle school, which is when peer relationships and identity issues are formative. She writes, "As diligent as parents are in their attempts to help their twins separate and individuate, identical twins struggle profoundly to discover their innermost selves. For some pairs, a physical separation can help create the emotional space necessary for psychological growth and maturation."[152]

As with most things that concern multiples, fraternals tend to be treated step-motherly also in this context. When the discussion turns to whether twins should be together or separated in school, the challenge for identical multiples seems to take center-stage.

Yet, parents of fraternals obviously also need to be aware of their children's need for time apart and to be seen as just the one. Researchers like Judy W. Hagedorn and Janet W. Kizziar (a duo of identical twins), who interviewed over 400 sets of twins, both identical and fraternal, say it might be trickier for fraternals to cope with society's comparisons, and when you think about it, it's obvious: identical multiples usually compete on fairly equal grounds, while in a duo or trio of fraternals one might continuously out-match the two others.

Hagedorn and Kizziar speculate to whether this could be a reason why so many fraternals decide to go their own separate ways early in life. Though they also add, as other researchers have noted, that parents of fraternals are more likely to allow the twins to develop in different directions since little attention just for being twins is afforded the two.[153]

May the best sister win (and also lose)

Now, let's have a look at how being in the same class as your siblings might play out. If you'd pass by our childhood living room one evening during the 1990s, you'd find three girls overly concerned about each other's toilet visits. At least that's how it may have appeared. At one point one of us would get up from her chair, prompting a wholly alarmed question from the others: "Where are you going?"

"To the bathroom!" the reply would come, followed by a mildly panicked:

"You're coming back, right?"

Even now, more than twenty years later, I recall the suspicion as one sister left the room. We knew the DNA was shared, so to ensure a fair competition, other conditions had also to be kept in check. A night off from studying before a test or exam had to be agreed on by all three, or even twenty minutes more. If one got up from the sofa to study just that little bit more, chances were the two others would groan and head back to the books. Looking back, it's somewhat surreal, but yes, extra study time without telling the others was perceived as actually cheating.

When I discovered the writings of David A. Hay, an Australian researcher who has studied the needs of multiples in school, my eyes widened. He argues, "Parental concern about differences between twins in their school achievement accentuates the feeling of inadequacy and differences between twins. There is no doubt that this is more of an issue for twins than for singletons, since academic achievements is not being compared with the whole school but simply with their twin."[154]

That was *precisely* it. My competitors were my sisters. Whenever I got a test result back as a child and teen, the results were still not in: I had to check-in with Mariann and Trude. If we all scored the same, that was fine, but not anything special, even if we all aced the test. If a freckle on a nose can make you a recognizable little person, then surely an A- and an A are a world apart. These seemingly inconsequential differences were honed in on and emphasized, just like when we got our test results back. The result was only star-dusted if I did better than them, if I had done something they couldn't do—*only me.*

Eventually, both I and the world noticed that I often got a few points more than Mariann and Trude. In hindsight it is easy to see that I ended up with those points in my favor simply because I worked that little bit harder. I could be "the smartest," a hard-won label I had to deliver on. My work had to be flawless. The competition was only a point behind.

As an adult I realize how annoying we must have been to our classmates. For pupils who were less academically inclined, it probably felt horrible when two of the three on top of the class groaned in disappointment at results far better than their own. Other children might have looked more gently on me if they'd been aware of the psychological elements behind all of this.

Hay notes, "The question is how to get across to the twins, their peers, the teachers and the parents that one twin is not 'dumb' (and that is the sort of derogatory term the adolescent uses) just because he or she does not do as well as the co-twin. This will apply even if the twins are first and second in the class, as one will be 'inferior' to the other."[155]

Let's pause Hay briefly so that I can properly convince you of the ludicrousness at play in the world's perception of multiples with this comment from the goldmine that is the Internet. On the comment section for a TV documentary on identical twins, an identical twin writes, *It is still now (at 48) very frustrating that people JUDGE us by what our sister does or is. I am now a Professor of Mathematics and Statistics at Melbourne University, she is a Medical Director at Pfizer in the US (...). By the way, I am the 'stupid' twin, although I am a nuclear physicist and I have a PhD in Applied Mathematics: she has always been the wise one.*[156]

Back to Hay. Sympathy, he argues, should be given to the twins in such a situation. The problem doesn't rest in them, he believes, but in the obvious comparisons between the twins that come with the school system of assessment and in the need to educate teachers, parents and peers to look at both twins as individuals, rather than as a duo.[157]

As researchers have noted, and like my sisters and I also did, many twins and triplets eventually vote with their feet and gratefully choose different classes at secondary schools or even different schools altogether.[158]

Multiples have a more driven quest for individuality than singletons

The comparisons become less when you're on your own. It did for us when we chose different classes in secondary school. One factor is the external pressure. If people don't know you're a multiple, then obviously there's no one for them to compare you with. But for my sisters and I, it wasn't relevant to compare either. Even if we all did the same level of math, English or geography, our research into who fared best with our shared DNA would be deeply flawed. Things had changed. Conditions weren't equal any longer, so *we* didn't have to be. One could have the better teacher, face an easier test, or simply not care that much. The pressure was off. The drive to excel at school was still there, but now the competition was finally with just *the one*.

I wasn't surprised when I learned that the quest for individuality is more driven in multiples than in others. Psychotherapist Barbara Klein says the road to individual identity for twins is hard won and often overdetermined. She reports that "once twins get a taste of independence and uniqueness they seem to hunger for more and more individuality."[159] So, when we start pulling apart, it seems to be a snowball that starts rolling. Much in the same vein, and in stark contrast to stereotypical beliefs about twins, multiples might be more fully aware of our uniqueness than others. Klein quotes Susan L. Farber, who studied twins reared apart. Farber argues that "twins [who grow up together], because they strive for individuality in such a determined manner, are not actually good subjects for the nature-nurture controversy."[160] And Klein sums it up, "What is truly interesting about twins is their struggle to become unique individuals as a reaction to being treated similarly in childhood and even adolescence. Struggles for distinct accomplishments are more highly charged than the struggles for identity in non-twins."[161]

I get that. It's a complicated, messy picture, but you're pulling apart while also ironically trying to keep up. You're two, three or even four people busy upping the idea of what's the normal threshold. The positive spin on this is of course how you show each other possibilities. It's the philosophical notion of how each of us sets our own limitations, but then realizing that in fact there are two other people busily broadening your canvas. Most people limit themselves based on their experiences and what they expect of themselves. As a multiple, chances are you're grown up with the message that you can do what your siblings can, which may or not be true, but either way you have two other people stretching those boundaries for you, showing you what also you might be capable of. It's standing on a dive platform, wondering if you should take the leap when you hear cheers from the pool down below. *"See, I did it! You can do it too!"* Or, before you've even had time to think, having someone take your hand and start the countdown for the jump.

On a side note, it's the day Trude and I cheered when Mariann jumped on water skis. "We can water ski jump!" we excitedly told each other. "Our body just did that!" The next day, I sucked at water skiing. My patient and wholly amused sisters insisted I try seventeen times (they meticulously kept count: *"Bah ha ha ha,* fifteen!") to get up from the water until Mariann's husband jumped into the water to literally lift me up and onto the skis.

But the idea remains: I still see water skiing (perhaps not jumping) as a possibility. If Mariann can learn how to do it, then so can I. Eventually. Maybe. At least my body can do it. Because you look at the others and expect that you can do what they can. Furthermore, you can't just be—you have to *do*. If you just *are*, then these other two are just like you. You have a need to find yourself beyond what most singletons go through.

How competition and comparisons may be flipped around as strengths in life

If you google self-awareness—as you obviously do if an executive development consultant highlights this in your feedback—the Internet tells you it's the same as self-knowledge. It's about understanding who you are, your strengths and flaws, how you got to be that way and how you affect others. It also ties in with emotional intelligence. As mentioned, I'm putting both squarely on being an identical multiple.

I also believe, perhaps somewhat paradoxically, that the continuous competition and comparisons with my sisters at one point morphed into a clear strength in life.

Throughout my teens, I had my sisters immediately give me feedback on anything and everything I did, didn't do, said or didn't say—a kind of 1990s beta version of social media like and dislike buttons. I also had a panoply of others eager to define me or let me know how they perceived me in comparisons to my sisters. Both aspects surely build a high level of self-awareness yet not necessarily self-esteem.

Yet, what I believe is of importance in the long-term is the complete honesty between three people when it comes to sharing thoughts and feelings.

We all want to go through life as full persons. Only rarely, however, do we see people as that, because we don't really share that deeply with each other. Perhaps because most of us would like others to think that we do things easily, and shy away from discussing openly any struggle, concern, fear or insecurity.

While I may at times cautiously ask questions of one of my friends or brothers, tip-toeing in case I'm getting close to anything that would be uncomfortable for them to speak about, I don't have this kind of filter with my sisters. There are also questions that it wouldn't feel right to ask anyone else than Mariann and Trude.

I think it makes me a better person by, at times, having certain realizations that others might never get, that clarity on what others might be going through and how your own thoughts might be more common than you think. That some thoughts are simply human. They're normally just unknown, unseen, unspoken of—unlike comparisons of multiples.

CHAPTER 13

How to make a shared birthday a child's very own

Let's start with a massive piece of good news: sharing a birthday isn't like sharing a piece of pie. A shared birthday can mean *more* birthday. Yet, an exponentially bigger birthday doesn't happen by chance. It happens because you have parents who take charge and make sure each child gets their fair share of attention. With lots of other twins' and triplets' most excellent birthdays and Christmases and Hanukahs in mind, here is a seven-point guide.

First, some reassurance. As surprising as this might be to any child, there comes a point in time when many adults start to shrug over birthdays.

"Oh, I don't like birthdays," they say.

Or, "Yeah, I'm not celebrating either,"

"It's nothing special. Just another day."

It's hard for children, who bubble over with energy on their big day, to fathom. On our big day three little girls fed off each other's excitement. We still do.

Over the years, whenever 16 May has appeared on our radar, my sisters and I have put our heads together to think of ways we could celebrate together. Who could take the train or fly over? Could we make it a long-weekend, and if our birthday fell mid-week, could we at least do a group call in the morning? Now, when we're all together in Oslo, we've started what we aim to make a long-lasting tradition of all taking the day off work to celebrate together.

"I've never thought much about the fact that I share a birthday with you," Mariann says. "On the contrary. You multiply the excitement when there are three children opening presents at the same time. We had two others to be excited with, to talk about what you wanted, and plan everything." She pauses a moment to think, then continues. "You know what, I think Mum and Dad were so good at making us feel that it was *our* special day, as in each of us, and that's why I never thought of it as little. Now, as an adult, it's extra special when we're able to see each other and have our birthday together, because it's not just my day, it's *our* day. Sharing a birthday for me means always having someone you'd love to celebrate with."

1. Let's start with what matters most for children: gifts

It's basic: Only rarely can bigger yet shared presents compete with having your *own* presents all to yourself, be they big or small, on your birthday or for Christmas. Group gifts are right up there with homework, liver stews, and long winters without snowfalls, whether you're a multiple, sibling, or simply someone who's inadvertently been roped into this weird phenomenon. Except when you're a multiple, when it seems to happen all the goddamn time.

"Don't you remember anything?" our aunt said as she looked at us with annoyance.

We looked back sheepishly, standing in her doorway, holding just the one present. We did remember, though we hadn't half an hour earlier when my sisters and I were roaming the local mall for potential birthday presents for her six-year-old twin boys. We'd set out to find two different gifts but impatience, mainly our father's, had quickly run thin.

"Can't we just get one larger one?" he'd suggested.

Deep down, we knew we were about to commit a twin transgression—against one of our own. Our reply was thus: "Okay, as long as it's *much* bigger."

Our father, sniffing a chance to get out of the mall, wrapped it up, "What about this one? Okay, let's pay. It's perfect."

But my aunt knew better. And so did we.

As Trude says, "Unless you're thinking of digging them a pool in the garden, skip the shared gift. Mum and Dad were good at this. We always got our own gifts. Things to share we got at other times, but not on our birthday or at Christmas."

Only once have I received a group gift on my birthday or for Christmas that I was dizzyingly happy with, a makeup head, framed by a long blonde wig with a tray of eyeshadows and lipsticks in front, a gift so big that my sisters and I knew that there was no way any of us would have received it on our own. "The makeup doll," as we so creatively called it, went to live in the room where my sisters and I kept most of our toys, until one day—there it was, the tragedy of the commons.

Someone had sealed the doll's fate with an irrevocable patchy haircut, which was meant to match the blue eyeshadow, colored roots, and orange lipsticked cheeks. No one had done it, no one had seen it happen. Also, there wasn't much to be said, as it wasn't just mine to do with as I pleased; it was *ours*, available to all. In other words, it was a free for all, simply having been stationed too far away from our own individual rooms where we kept our most prized possessions (all of which were our very own).

Now if I, a triplet, can pass on a shared gift to a set of twins, a lot of other people out there might seriously mess this up. Thus, as a parent, you should tell guests to remember to bring one for each, and if you fear some will find it too expensive to buy three presents at a time, tell them to simply scale down their budget. Give them a shared gift any other day of the year. We had lots of them as children and they were brilliant: all the board games, the massive play kitchen fully equipped with plastic vegetables, pretty much all our books. Well, almost all our books.

"I remember a year we invited to a big birthday party—we must have been five or six years old," Mariann says. "There was this one girl that had been invited by me, so she thought she should bring *one* present, for me. I remember the other girls made a bit fun of her because she hadn't properly wrapped the present. She had just put it in a bag. But inside was a book, and I remember how cool it was because it was just for me. It was a present *just* for me." At this point, Mariann has to pause because she is laughing so hard. "You didn't get any. Just me. It was the coolest present of the entire birthday. Because it was just mine."

"So, I didn't get a present?"

Mariann, still laughing, says "No. Only me!"

And, when your twins or triplets head to someone else's birthday, let them each bring a gift. Giving a gift is a social skill, almost on par with excitement in receiving one's own. You want to set the example here; you can't ask other parents to have their child bring along three gifts for your children if you later treat them as a group yourself and send them along with a shared gift in return.

2. The "Normal Siblings Test" will put it right

My sisters and I would have successfully navigated that gift buying for our cousins if we had run the conundrum through the "Normal Siblings Test." It's straightforward: imagine a strange coincidence in which your five-year-old and six-year-old both have birthdays on the same day. And if you're a triplet parent, toss in an eight-year-old too.

For convenience's sake you're throwing them a shared birthday party. As a parent you'd be over yourself with creativity, trying to figure out how to make sure each of these little people get their own celebratory moment as, after all, they already share their birthday. If you were a guest you'd be just as keen to make sure that these two or three didn't have to share more than necessary. You'd make sure they, as with all other children, felt that they were the center of the universe for that one day.

Now, up that experience of sharing to a whole lot more and a lot more frequently than just a birthday and you have the story of twins and triplets, as well as a strong reminder why you really should focus on the individuals on their big day.

3. In addition to separate gifts, let them have their own cake and song too

Sing "Happy Birthday" as many times as there are children. Twins? Twice. Triplets? Three times? Quads? Yes, four times. These children have waited a whole year for this day, so everyone else can wait a few minutes longer for cake and yes, sing that song again. And again. A joint "Happy Birthday *KariMariannTrude*" is fine for Kari who's first, but not so cool for whoever's the one who's always mentioned last in the group listing, even on her birthday. (Indeed, it seems uniquely to be the one with the longest name).

Also, one person—one cake. In short: it's remarkably more fun to be asked to blow out candles on a cake if someone else doesn't beat you to it. If you're the baking kind of parent, go for the full-sized chocolate cakes or whatever flavor your children fancy. If you're a baking-shirker like myself, divide one cake into three and decorate differently. Or make one large one with an anagram of their initials in smarties and opt for candles on individual cupcakes.

4. Help them hold onto the excitement

We wrap presents to build up excitement. For a minute or two, a child struggling with a ribbon is figuring out a secret; they're a few seconds away from finding out.

Although, that would be a few seconds too late. Right then, a sister would shout out from across the room: "We got dolls!" Then the other sister would chime in: "Ooooh, dolls! I got a green one! What did you get?!"

Uhm. I don't know yet, but I presume a doll with a different colored dress than green?

"We knew that we would get identical presents," Trude says, "so it was a matter of opening them up insanely quickly, so we would also *know* at the same time. It was annoying to open after you and already know what we'd gotten. We got quite good at unwrapping fast though, because you still wanted to open yours before the others."

That, my dear reader, is why we come up with rules in this society. Chances are your children will quickly come up with their own, but if they need some ideas here are a few that have been developed, tested and tried by a panel of little triplets:

- 1-2-3: We counted. When everyone had one of those identical-looking presents in hand, we'd count out loud. *Oooonee... twooo... three!* And by the count of three we'd start unpacking and if the tape and ribbon was on your side, you'd finish around the same time as these other two.

- Big presents, different rules: For important presents, and that would be any big ones if you're a child, we'd sit with our backs turned to each other. No one could say out loud what we got. It was fine to cheat your sisters from a bit of excitement on the small things, but on the big ones, we brought out the big rules.

- Get creative with the gifts but hands off the wrapping! To all the clever clogs who gave us identical presents wrapped differently, I still remember you. It utterly ruined the system. As what I can only presume was a nod to the idea that opening a present is half the fun, some and I shall not mention names, figured it would be great to add a ball of bubble wrap in one, a bit of cardboard in another and a kitchen towel in the third. Little did they know that only identical presents would always be opened at the same time, different looking ones could at times be opened at random. So, by the time my second sister had opened hers, I'd feel a twinge of disappointment as I was then quickly handed mine: 'Oh, you might as well open your present now then.'

5. Go crazy—try *different* presents

I've become a well-meaning aunt myself. When birthdays or Christmas draw near, I call my brother. What works for a seven-year-old? What is my niece into now? What should I get to make her happy? Admittedly, at times I've given up. I've transferred money to my brother and asked him to choose and wrap something on my behalf.

Thus, I fully sympathize with the ones who gave up in the face of finding three thoughtful presents. Also, they probably figured they'd give a pass to potential situations where a child would peek at her sisters' presents and think they got the better ones. So we got the same, or they jazzed it up a bit with different colors.

Yet, the way I see it, identical presents is a missed opportunity to teach multiples that fair does not always mean identical. Because around the three identical sets of hats, stockings, dolls and bikes also grew an expectation of absolute equality. And when you're an inhabitant of a world where everything is seemingly the same, that becomes what constitutes "fair."

Yet, here's a truth Joan A. Friedman (you know, the twin psychologist I have a crush on), says she continuously repeats:

we cannot make life fair and equal for each twin. The preoccupation with fairness, she argues, locks twins in constant battles with one another and makes them continuously police what the other is getting or doing. She asks, "How will they learn to handle the uncontrollable environmental variables that will ultimately creep into their lives?"[162]

It's a question I suspect many parents are aware of, yet still stuck on. Like my own parents were. Here's what my father said when I asked how they maneuvered this: "We often faced the challenge that you're three individuals and at the same time you're similar. Just imagine, if we had bought new shoes for two of you and not the third, there would have been a massive protest. We wouldn't have managed to deal with that. So we were very conscious that you would get the same. We also made care that Stig should also get it then, so he wouldn't feel left out. We had four to take care of when it came to buying things, whether clothes or toys. We did have the philosophy that everyone should be treated equally, and we needed first and foremost to avoid any kind of jealousy between you. That was what was in the back of our minds all the time."

Touché, I thought when he said that. It seemed, I'm sorry Dad, quite similar to an anecdote Friedman tells, one she calls "tragic" about a mother who was "hopelessly controlled by her daughters' need for absolute equality." It's also a story about shoes: "[T]he mom could not fathom buying a pair of shoes for one daughter if she needed them without buying a pair for the other. The mother could not tolerate the ensuing relentless battle cry—"It's not fair."[163]

Now, to get out of our rut of what's fair, we need a different kettle of fish altogether. Only as an adult does it strike me how

PARENT LIKE A TRIPLET

different our gift receiving scenario was from what most people experience. Sure, at times two brothers might get the same thing, like in our family where every year one of our uncles got each of us five children a big marzipan pig. But show me the family where two sisters or three brothers get the same from everyone for every birthday and every Christmas, and I'll wager they're twins or triplets, and more so identical ones.

Trude says, "We never got anything specifically for us personally. Everyone got a radio, or everyone got drawing kits, or everyone got a pair of trousers. I didn't think about it at the time, but I do now when you're writing this book and I'm more conscious about this whole thing. The thing with being seen for who you are—we didn't have that on our birthday. It's natural that children have a wish list and tell you what they want, but if you're going to buy for three and they are to get the same, then you can't really match gifts with personality or interest."

Trude continues, "But then again, how creative are children in their wishes when they're eight? They want a ball. But there was a never a question of giving us a doll, a remote-controlled car, and a watch. Then we all would get that car. It was probably done deliberately to not treat us differently, and it was probably practical. We all had identical gym bags, all the same jackets. But Stig was in this equation too. It's not always easy to separate what's due to being siblings versus being a triplet. Stig also often ended up with the same as us, but if Stig got something, was it just as important that we got it? I'm asking for a friend—*ha ha ha*. It might feel more unfair if three gets something and one doesn't, versus if just he got something."

Trude adds, "I only have great, wonderful memories from birthdays and Christmases. The thing with gifts—it's only something I thought about now as an adult. I never thought about it when little."

"Yeah," I say dryly, "do you know why? Because you wanted a Walkman."

"Yes! And you didn't? *Ha ha ha*. There you go."

Christmas at eleven came with Walkmans: it was that year's present from Mum and Dad, the biggest present of the year, and the one I looked forward to for just as long. After all the presents had been opened, my father pulled me aside for a one-to-one. I still remember what he said: "I saw that you got disappointed, Kari. We know you wanted a camera. You'll get that next year."

I felt mortally ashamed. I felt ungrateful and guilty for not being able to hide my disappointment. A Walkman was, after all, a splendid present. I also knew that a camera, let alone three, was a bit out of reach money-wise. Yet I still felt immensely disappointed, not because I hadn't gotten specifically what I wanted but because I had gotten what my sisters specifically had asked for when I didn't even want it. There were three of us and we always got the same... it just didn't seem fair.

6. Include—and exclude—twins and triplets like you would another child

What if only one of your twins or two of your triplets are invited to a party. Is that okay? Yes and no. Life isn't always fair or equal or the same, however you perceive those categories, and as with the gift giving, it's fine for twins and triplets to learn that at a young age. Fortunately, normal rules in society apply.

Thankfully most kindergartens and schools operate with clear-cut rules: You either go for *all* the children, *all* the girls, *all* the boys, or if you're to make a narrower selection, you make sure it's an obvious group, like the ones living close by or the girls in the dance group, so you don't randomly exclude a few. Today, inviting the token twin or triplet would hopefully not fly.

From we were seven to ten, one of our classmates put in a rotating schedule for the triplets. When I missed her birthday party one year, I was gutted. The next two years, her invitations would skip my desk, as well as one of my sister's, only to be handed to the third.

"I remember I once said, 'I wonder if it's because she thinks she's just getting one present,'" Mariann says. "Mum got incredibly angry and said she'd always taken great care to make sure we always gave different presents. Mum thought a lot and really tried hard to not let others perceive us a group, but like three different ones with three different gifts. It was never a gift from 'the triplets.' It was from Trude, Mariann, and Kari. And I remember, I really regretted saying it out loud."

Obviously, adults need to step in if children randomly exclude just one or two; if not, what signals do we send to the children being excluded or the ones being allowed to exclude just a few? But, if your children are excluded like any other children would be in their situation, however, be it because only one twin plays football and his team's keeper is turning eleven, or it's the birthday of a classmate of only one of the multiples, then maybe it's a chance for you to have some alone time with the other.

7. Shared guests or each their guests?

In some cases, birthday invitations are straightforward. If your children live in a small community, play with the same children in the neighborhood, go to the same school, or are in the same class and even do the same after school activities, it's a shared one. Assigned guests can quickly become divisive both for the ones having to navigate "Whose friend is it really?" as well as for the ones being invited by one specific twin or triplet: "Whose guest am I?" or "But what if I like her better—am I 'yours' now?" and "Do I need to choose between you?"

If your children are in separate classes, attend different activities, and their friends are clearly either shared or individual, then a mix of shared invites and personal invites seems sensible. Along with individual invites, of course, comes just one gift. But for that to work in a shared birthday party, you need to make sure each twin or triplet has the same amount of people (read: gifts).

One mother of triplets suggested this method: each child gets to invite five other children. State specifically that the invitation is from *that* specific child. Ask friends to RSVP so if one can't attend, your children can invite one more to ensure they all have the same number of friends in attendance and thus bring a gift to that person. The gifts even out.

CHAPTER 14

She's the pretty one: dealing with physical comparisons

When you go about this world with your very own measuring sticks, comparisons are easy and inevitable—for both you and the world. Yet, the fact that simply being a *twin* increases your chances of an eating disorder should make parents jump into instant alert mode and do what they can to downplay the abundant comparisons, especially of looks.

While most children won't really pause to look at their bodies and many a teenager will do their best to avoid mirrors, growing up I saw my body all the time: on Mariann and Trude.

Most twins and triplets are on the same routines when little. Whenever you're brushing those teeth, it's also time for those siblings of yours to do the same. The mirror wasn't that big in our bathroom, and we would squeeze together so that we could all see. We stood there, shoulder to shoulder to shoulder, mostly brushing those teeth but also looking from one sister to the next. At times we would encourage each other to continue to stare into the mirror even after the teeth were brushed. Mirrors don't offer a 360-degree view, but a sister does.

Sometimes we would demand that the two others turn around. "I'd like to see," one of us would say, and if the others were in a good mood, they would comply.

Reasons were two-fold. One was curiosity, how do they—and I—look? And the other down to other people's curiosity: What were people likely to point out when they met us all?

Fast-forward some thirty years and Trude and I exchange a quick glance.

"Your face is a bit rounder."

It's not so much the comment itself that surprises me but the setting. We're in my son's kindergarten, talking with the most senior member of the staff, a white-haired woman that I adore and from whom I hungrily crave parenting advice.

Seriously, did you just say that? You too?! runs through my mind. Instead I say, "Eh yeah... she's seven months pregnant."

"Oh," the woman replies, laughing, "I didn't see it at first."

We laugh it off too. Trude is indeed holding my son, a ninety-centimeter decoy in front of her protruding stomach, but I can't help but think to myself, *Yes, but you didn't really need a second look before you started comparing us.*

Now, mere seconds before the comparison, the kindergarten teacher gushed: "Gosh, you're similar. We always think she's you!"

All good. If my son's beloved kindergarten teacher had stopped there, it would have been a lovely conversation. While I've yet to appreciate comparisons, I take it as a compliment whenever someone says I look like Mariann or Trude, at least from most people.

In the entrance to our home, I've put up a few photos, including two of me and our son. For months he stubbornly pointed to one of these and said, 'Auntie Trude!' whenever my husband or Trude lifted him up to see. Which happened often, as they both found the confusion hilarious.

I didn't. I know it's silly, and that it's probably even logical that a one and a half-year old says two photos next to each other are of different people, but it irked me, and perhaps even more so whenever Trude said he'd picked out the one with the widest grin as her.

People often forgo all common sense when speaking with multiples

Sitting at a cafe later that day, Trude and I discuss how comparisons are much harsher when you're in your teens and told that one tooth is slightly different to your sisters', that you walk a bit more manly, that your bum is larger—all told up-front in the neutral manner that befalls people when they dissect the looks of multiples, finding differences where they expect there to be none. We talk about, for example, how compliments that are in fact unabashed comparisons would be unthinkable outside the triplet context.

"Oh, you're the pretty one!" Trude says. "People think it's a compliment. I remember the French colleague of Mariann told me that. *How rude!*, I thought—talking down my sisters. Why give a compliment with a reference to someone else? Tell someone that they're better looking than their sister? Why can't I be good looking, full stop? Why can't I be smart, full stop? Why make it relative?"

Trude goes on. "I have a friend with a sister who's not good looking. It wouldn't even cross my mind to tell my friend that she's the prettier sister. It's something we experience, but no one else. If people are to get this, they need to put it through the sibling test: if you're looking at two sisters, would you tell them, while they're both there, that one is prettier? Or tell one of them afterwards, 'I think you're the prettiest of you two'? No, you wouldn't. Because that would be insanely rude, and people would think why in the world are you bringing my sister into this?"

"Uhm, do people tell you that you're the pretty one?" I ask.

"Yes. They don't say that to you?"

"No."

"*Muah ha ha ha ha.*"

Here's what's worrying: being a twin increases the risk of an eating disorder

One pea, two peas, three peas in a pod. Among the twin clichés we find the competing, anorexic twins who count peas.

Unfortunately, there's truth in the stereotype: twin studies suggest a genetic link. If anorexia is partly based in biology, it makes sense that the risk of both twins getting ill is higher for identicals (who share all their genes) than for fraternals (who share genes typical of any siblings). One study attributes more than half of the risk of developing anorexia to genes.[164] Other studies have shown that if an identical twin has an eating disorder, the other twin is more than two times likely to have an eating disorder as well. For fraternal twins, the risk of the other twin developing it is around one-tenth of the likeliness.[165]

However—and this is the part to really worry about—simply *being a twin* puts you at risk. A Swedish study that followed more than two million children from birth and into their teens and young adult years found that twins and triplets were 33 percent more likely to be diagnosed with anorexia later in life compared to singletons.[166]

The finding baffled researchers; it was counter-intuitive. The study also showed that having non-twin siblings tends to shield you from eating disorders. The twin conundrum held even after the researchers considered other factors like prematurity or a mother who smokes.

The media coverage on this research ran with the idea of a "natural mirror" for identical twins, setting the stage for intense comparisons and competitiveness.[167] But, as far as I could tell, the study didn't specify twin type, yet all the media accounts did. The study simply said "twins." I was curious; was the finding "identical twins" or "all twins"?

I ask because while researching this book, it has increasingly dawned on me that the world of fraternals and identicals often overlap. Most fraternals face the same challenges as identicals. You're compared not to a panoply of others but to just the one or two. While minute differences between identicals bring out the magnifying glasses, I'm not sure it's necessarily easier when the question of who's tallest, thinnest, or better-looking is more clear-cut. Also, fraternals may go through puberty, the prime moment for developing a disturbed relationship with food and body, at different times, which is not likely to make comparisons easier to handle.

I asked Anna Goodman, one of the Stockholm researchers, whether the study distinguished between fraternals and identicals; *it didn't*. She had, however, been able to distinguish between twins of the same sex and twins of different sexes. And, she wrote, there was a slightly related matter she had looked at but that didn't make it into the final paper: Did the effect differ according to the sex of the twin?

It didn't.

Unfortunately, in the study it's a detail tucked into a table in the study's appendix. If you ask me, it should be front and center. This study, the largest and most comprehensive such study done to date, shows that whether same-sexed or not, fraternal or identical, *twins* run a higher risk of developing anorexia. Not identical twins. *Twins.*

Now, the question is obviously, "Why?" Unfortunately, the study doesn't say anything about the mechanisms at play. Eating disorders are complex, and there are a multitude of reasons that may lead someone down that particularly self-destructive path. Among the factors known to increase the risk, however, is a focus on body size and looks, ideals of thinness, and dieting.[168]

You're aware that you're on display

When I see twins, I deliberately ignore them. Although I'm as curious as the next (or maybe even more as I'm both a triplet myself and writing this book), I make a conscious effort not to look, as I know that most other people won't think twice about doing so. Because while adult multiples may remember well what it feels like as a child to be stared at, most other people won't, as few people spend much of their childhood being scrutinized by strangers.

To give you an idea, let's peek into a red Peugeot in a ferry parking lane. Oh, it's okay to look—everyone else is. My sisters and I are six years old. We're strapped into the car's backseat and we're staring straight ahead, bored and uncomfortable.

The ferry we're waiting for is nowhere to be seen. In the cars parked on both side of ours, it feels like everyone, whether seated in the back seats or front seats, is looking at us.

Then Trude steps up on her throne of legendary greatness. Seated to my right, next to one of those unfortunate windows, she turns her head as fast as only an indignant six-year-old can manage, biting her eyes into the woman in the car opposite ours. The woman jumps in her seat, slumps back, and retracts her stare, as does everyone else. As far as I'm concerned, it's the world's greatest payback. As far as our parents are concerned, there could be less awkwardness in the lanes. Mariann and I roar with laughter, Trude looks eminently pleased, and our parents are doing their best to calm us. "People have to be allowed to look at you," I recall Dad saying, while Mum said, "*Hushhh*, girls." But there and then, all I was thinking was, *Yes, just like we can look at them!*

While your co-multiples are likely to multiply your cuteness and you might at times relish the attention you get, most multiples eventually realize that the cards are stacked against them. It's the simple but important difference between being *seen* and being *known*. The attention is steered your way because you form part of a duo or trio, not because of *you*, because on your own, well, no one really looks at you. Walk down the street without your co-multiples and you're a mere mortal like everyone else but have them next to you and people will not only look, they will let you know what they think of *how* you look—and *how you look in comparison*.

When we started going out as teenagers, we got ready together. We'd bring a radio into the bathroom, pool our make-up, and cram in front of the mirror. We brought our faces close and looked at what worked and not when it came to the makeup and hair, and whether one sister had fared better that evening.

"I remember that you two were better at putting on makeup," Mariann says of those days. "I would get upset if you wouldn't do mine, because of course I didn't want to be the ugly one. I wanted to be the one who looked the same."

This is also why any premature suggestions of a mirror line-up would be shot down. If you finished a bit before your sisters or were particularly pleased with how you looked that evening, you might be tempted to ask a tad too early, "Can you come here? I want to have look."

More often than not, the reply would be a flat-out "no," perhaps with a short, sour explanation: "Don't even bother. I know what you want." Indeed, the last thing you want in the world is to let a sister use you as her "before" photo.

A dual challenge: wanting to be unique, but also the same

Every twin or triplet out there is aware that others will compare, so you end up with the dual challenge of wanting to look the same to not provide fodder for comparisons, to not let one upstage the other, and to want to look just like you.

An identical twin battling an eating disorder says, "I'm staring at my beautiful sister and she was always skinnier than I was. We're twins; I know we should look alike, but I don't feel like I look as pretty as she does."[169]

A set of twins facing anorexia and bulimia say, "Our goal as twins is to look identical, so we don't have people saying 'Oh, you're the bigger twin.'"[170]

It's like the story Mariann reminded me of during another cafe date. She mentioned an episode with a boyfriend in her early twenties, saying, "He had seen the three of us on the other side of the subway station, and when we met up, he commented on how my bum was twice as big as yours."

"What?! Oh my god."

"I think it was his way of encouraging me to work out more."

"But you were really tiny!"

"You guys were what, 61 kilos, and I was maybe 64 kilos. Not only was it a mean thing to say, but it also proved to me how little he knew me. I think his comment hit me harder than it would have hit most people if they had been compared with a sibling, because I've been compared my entire life with you two. I had worked so hard to become my own person. There and then all I could think was, *I need to break this off, this isn't working*."

Another twist on unbidden comparisons is being repeatedly told you don't look like yourself but more like your sister. Perhaps you're mid-conversation on a topic, any topic, and this type of comment churns up (more often than you'd think with people who know us well): "Do you know what? I've always thought you and Trude looked the most alike, but now I actually think you and Mariann are much more similar."

Take it from me, these are not the best compliments if you thought you looked particularly good that day. Admittedly, it felt a bit unnecessary *on my own wedding day*. (I shall not name names, but I'll share the comment neither Mariann nor I were overly happy with: "You look gorgeous, Kari! You don't really look like yourself though, but Mariann really looks like you today!" Uhm, thanks. Two brief sentences, two triplets offended.)

As an adult, I reply a neutral, "Okay" and resume the topic we'd been focused on, but as a child and teenager I didn't say anything. I really thought I had to hear people out, despite how divisive and confusing it felt. I wanted to look different and have people be able to tell me apart, and be seen for me, but if there was to be a line-up, I'd rather not be the one pointed to as the *different* one. When my sisters were deemed to look more similar, I felt like I had failed. At the same time, as I wanted to just be me, I needed to get this triplet thing *right.*

Perhaps it was because when one was singled out, it normally came with a lengthy explanation of why; you were the odd one out, the one who needed to be justified. Maybe it was also because the singled-out triplet would often be the one that was slightly "rounder." Show me an insecure teenager who's happy with that.

I truly understand why many multiples dislike being together in photos. Why give people more opportunities to compare? If you befriend me on Facebook, you'll see that I have several photos of me and *one* of my sisters. I have, however, very few of all three. Perhaps because we know well that photos together of all three inevitably means comparisons.

"You always do this! You did this last year as well." And that would be Mariann for the second year in the running. Really, she should have known better and that was probably why Trude and I laughed so hard we held our stomachs.

"You tricked me!" Mariann continued. "I asked if you were getting dressed up and you said no."

Trude and I protested. "You should have assumed we'd put on mascara."

Every year, we head home to our father's house for Christmas, and the day before Christmas Eve we head out into the forest to get a Christmas tree. Mariann wasn't particularly concerned about going into a forest without make-up but about heading onto Facebook next to her sisters wearing make-up for hundreds of people to like and comment upon. You see, the previous year, several photos from our tree hunt had indeed been shared with the world.

What's with you Mariann. Why do you look so different? one person asked when he saw the photo. In all honesty, she didn't look all that different; she'd simply given a pass on mascara and filling in her blonde eyebrows.

We never posted that photo of our second round of Christmas tree hunting on Facebook. A triplet agreement was hashed out: everyone must be happy with the way they look if we are to be next to each other in online photos for all to see—and comment upon.

So, what can you do as a parent, neighbor, friend or anyone in the social circle of multiples?

1. Don't automatically comment on the children's appearance.

Children are cute. Yet, we don't have to always tell them that. It's a general point psychologists make: don't greet a child with comments about their body or appearance. Because what do the children then learn? Appearance matters. It creates a consciousness about the body, 'I see your body and it's important. It tells me who you are'.[171]

I'd argue that it's doubly important to keep those comments in check when it comes to multiples. There will simply be more of those comments around, whether it's, "Oh, aren't you cute," "Wow, you guys look similar," or "Am I seeing double/triple?" Moreover, repeatedly being told you look like someone else isn't particularly interesting to hear; it's being told apart that enhances a child's sense of self.

2. Make line-ups go beyond looks.

Most often in life, people are well-meaning. It's the neighbor or aunt who rehearsed on the way over. *Now, how was it again? Kari and scar, Trude and mole, Mariann and nothing.* And, frankly, a line-up makes things easier; that's why police use it. So often when a visitor came around, we'd find ourselves standing alongside each other. Often, we'd even suggested the line-up ourselves, demanding that guesses be kept on hold until all three were summoned. Not surprising, as we were repeatedly told, "If only I had all three of you in front of me, I would be able to tell you apart, but on your own? There's no chance."

Hopefully, there are some characteristic features about each person in your duo or trio you can share with people to make it easier to pin the right name on the right child. Yet, even if it's a matter of fraternals and the question is, "Who's the blonde one and who's the brown-haired one again?" or identicals with smaller differences, encourage people to go beyond looks when they greet your children. Rather than again asking for the scar, why not try a question that might even help them start a conversation with your children:

- "I'm really glad to see you. Now, help me with your names. I want your name and your favorite animal."
- "Hi girls. Mariann first, then Kari and then Trude: What's your favorite book/ice cream flavor/animal/etc.?"

Of course, most people will forget whether the child prefers blue or orange minutes after the question is asked, but it doesn't matter; it was a little shift of focus, of something nice being said that wasn't about appearance, a little message that it's not what they look like that matters. It's what they think, what they like, who they are.

3. Go fuss-free: just ask them, keep calm and carry on with the conversation.

"People keep mixing them up and asking them what their name is. Are they bothered by it?" a triplet mother asked me once. I was just about to answer, "Well, that depends on your children" when I remembered myself at age nine. It's not about the question itself, it's about the conversation that follows that question.

Life is straightforward when you're a child. A neighbor who stops to say hi and shoots in a quick question about who you are is simply a person making sure they know who they're speaking with. "Now, who do we have here?", "Which one are you of the girls?", "Is it Kari, Trude, or Mariann that's out for a walk?" These are all perfectly fine questions, ones I even appreciated, as I knew then that it mattered to them whom they were speaking to. They wanted to make sure they knew it was *me*.

The best adults stopped right there, pocketed the answer, and steered the conversation toward more exciting topics.

Unfortunately, life's more complicated when you're an adult. We feel like we need to explain. Instead of moving the conversation onto my new bike, this day's dinner or what I was up to that afternoon, I sometimes found myself quacking on about my sisters and our looks. I followed the thread because that's what you do as a child when adults ask you leading questions. "Yes that's true, it's easier to tell us apart when we're next to each other," "Yes, we do look very similar," and "No, they're inside, but it would have made it easier for you if they were here."

Thus, if faced with multiples, know that it's great that you want to be sure whom you're talking with, that it's fine to ask, but then to do as the Brits: keep calm and carry on. It's the friendly chat the children are after, not the dissection of looks.

4. Don't search hard for new differences. At least not out loud.

Chances are the children know well what visual differences people use to tell them apart. However, you should make sure to not go searching for more characteristics, at least not out loud in front of the children.

The challenge at hand, however, is that since the children themselves might already have pointed enthusiastically to a distinct characteristic, many won't think twice about adding a few more: "Yes, and you seem to have a slightly rounder face," or "Your hair is longer," or "Are you a bit shorter?"

As a child, I realized that it was all done with the best of intentions, that people were trying to remind themselves of what characteristics went with whom. "Yeah, I see that the two of you are... and you're a bit more...". But, what they ended up doing was pointing out minuscule differences, and they did so out loud, placing emphasis on what otherwise would go unnoticed.

5. Scrap the comparisons at home. Let them just be themselves.

If you're a parent of multiples, consider your home a comparison-free zone. While the world will compare what your children do, how they seem and how they look, you can make sure they're seen for just themselves while at home.

People change, but labels often stick, so let them figure out who they are on their own. As a twin parent said, "As a parent, you should quickly do what you can to embrace what makes them unique in a positive light and get into the habit of protecting them from the abundant outside comparisons they will receive."[172]

CHAPTER 15

Build a bond with each child and between your singleton(s) and multiples

Being the older or younger sibling of twins or triplets is not necessarily all Sound of Music. Worried parents who suddenly find themselves divvying up their attention in ever smaller slices will find much reassurance in this piece, in which I tell you to treat your children like you would a singleton and spend time one-on-one with each. (Keep on breathing and reading, you got this). And, although many older siblings find the influx of siblings challenging, they may still grow close, at least as adults.

Whenever I ask my brother Tord, who is older by eight years, what it was like to grow up with triplets or even with four younger siblings, he laughs it off.

"You really don't want to hear my version! Or we at least need a night with lots of wine, *ha ha ha.*"

A few times my father has commented on these conversations, saying, "I know Tord tells the story like we suddenly didn't see him, but I don't think that was the case. One of the problems when you have twins or triplets is that it's so much work with the babies, whom you need to help, and then it is as if your other children grow up in an instant. It's automatic that you give more attention to the triplets. Tord often managed on his own, while Stig was just two years old."

My father's comments make me think of another conversation I had with him about our triplet stroller, which—he seemed genuinely happy about this—attracted lots of attention, perhaps because getting us out and about as babies literally meant all hands on deck.

"The blue stroller we used when you were babies was incredibly heavy and difficult to maneuver. When we travelled by ferry [this is coastal Norway, so any journey to see relatives included at least one if not two ferries], we needed help from several people to carry it in, and then of course we were to bring in three babies as well."

When my father told me this story, I laughed, not because of the image of the three babies being handed to strangers but because my brothers are nowhere to be seen in this story. It's like the feat was already so massive that the fact that my parents also brought along a two- and an eight-year-old was a mere detail that wouldn't add much more to his story.

There's limited thrill in being "the sibling of the twins"

The addition of twin and triplet siblings to a family turns most children's lives upside down, and parents worry their singleton kids will feel left out, rejected, or excluded when they suddenly have to balance their time between, well, multiple children. Add to this the fact that whenever the family is out and about, these interlopers will receive attention remarkably out of proportion with their own. As one parent noted, "While we are doing everything that we can to reassure our singletons of their importance in our lives, the attention that is naturally drawn to multiple infants can send a different message."[173]

On one such day when our parents wheeled out the conspicuous triplet pram, two-year-old Stig had enough. As yet another stranger *bravo*-ed the trio in the pram, our parents suddenly heard the gawker yelp: Stig had kicked her as hard as he could. No one had even seen him; they only saw the triplets.

Thinking of my brothers—especially Tord, who was an only child for six years before the time and attention doted on him was suddenly cut into slices—and all other siblings of multiples, I recognize the considerable irony that I'm the one penning a book centering so much on the challenges of getting and demanding *too much* attention as a multiple.

Although my parents tried to cope with the conflicting demands of their children and lavish attention on all five, there were times when they clearly came up short. The prime contender is Tord's confirmation at fifteen, a ritual most teens in Norway eagerly sign up for, not really to confirm any Christian faith but to get the party, gifts, and a day that's supposedly all about them. I say "supposedly," because this is what Tord recalls: "You forgot me! Seriously, I walked home alone! On my own day!"

He laughs in near disbelief while recounting the story, as does my father who shakes his head and protests. "*Nooo*, we didn't. You were supposed to go with uncle Erlend, no?" After the church event, which was attended by many of our family members and friends, we returned home in cars. Well, most of us. One stayed behind in the parking lot.

The local newspaper came around later that day. Admittedly, I'm not sure whether to feel sad or to laugh whenever I see the newspaper clipping from Tord's big day, replete with a photo of three little girls grinning widely in their Norwegian national costumes while just behind them stands a boy twice their height in a suit, his smile absent (his glumness no doubt a lingering aftereffect of what happened earlier that day in the parking lot). *Triplets in confirmation*, the headline reads, while the caption rubs it in deeper: "Triplets Kari, Trude and Mari-ann Ertresvåg (7) are due to start school this fall. This weekend they attended the confirmation of their brother Trond."

Trond. Tord's big day wasn't even his.

"That is absolutely horrific," I once told him. "How in the world did Mum say okay to that story?"

"Who do you think called the newspaper?" he replied flatly.

Researcher Audrey C. Sandbank say siblings of twins often feel deprived because they are not one of the twins.[174] I get that. Out and about, they're, as one researcher frankly puts it, a "nonperson in the public eye,"[175] the ones patiently waiting by the supernova pram for anyone to also notice them. Then, at home, they're the sibling of a "group" they're not actually part of, a group seemingly bound by closeness and wallowing in attention.

It's like my brother's experience on what turned out not to be his day after all, and this bittersweet quote by a five-year-old brother of twins: "The twins have got each other. Mum and Dad have got each other. All I have got is the dog and he smells."[176]

So what do you do?

Thankfully, much of the advice in this book benefits singletons in a family of multiples, as parents should seek to downplay the status as multiples and treat their children more equally. In short, as best as you can, treat all your children like you would any singleton.

<u>1. Introduce your singleton in his or her own right, not always as the 'big brother of the twins'.</u>

As one parent notes in a twin forum, parents need to go a step beyond simply telling thoughtless strangers and friends to include their singleton(s) whenever someone stops to marvel at their young multiples. She'd once commented to her eight-year-old that the additional attention from friends and strangers due to the twins also meant that *he* got more attention.

Her son, however, had noticed something she hadn't. "People always included him in on the conversation but they always asked things like, How does it feel to have twins? Are you a big helper now that the twins are here? etc. He said people always asked him about the twins and never just about him. Then I realized that whenever he was asked anything the twins were always thrown in there with the question."[177]

Traditional gender roles, however, seem to come into play. In an Australian study, researcher Audrey C. Sandbank found that older brothers to a greater extent than older sisters disliked their young twin siblings, felt overshadowed and pushed out. Older sisters were more likely to enjoy being the twins' big sister and to use them as a way of getting extra attention for themselves.[178]

Nonetheless, it's a small and easy shift to put in place as a parent. Simply ditch introductions like "...and this is the twin's big brother, George" or "...and the twins are really lucky to have such a great older sister as Suzy" for "...and this is George, he's three and loves dinosaurs" and "...Suzy here is four years old and a right little monkey who we're now taking to the playground, so she can climb trees. Bye!".

2. Don't reinforce the distinction between the 'group' and the odd-one out.

If you opt for treating your children as you would any singleton, you won't continuously remind the one or two non-multiples that there's a package deal at home they're not part of.

If you call your children by their name rather than falling back on the shorthand "the twins" or "the triplets," they're all equal; it's not "George and the twins."

Similarly, if you dress them all differently, it's not the visible duo and the odd-one-out.

3. One-on-one time—with older siblings and with each of your multiples.

Now, before we go on, here's a message to any parent reading his: You know that quiet sigh you're about to let out? Take a deep breath instead, pour yourself a cup of tea, and hear me out.

First, let me say that I felt a twinkle of *touché* as I encountered the sigh of a mother of quadruplets and a singleton in an article on the impact of twins on siblings. "Like other parents," it reads, "the Harrimans have always made special efforts to give Andrew [their single-ton] exclusive time and to take him on outings alone. 'But now the quads realize that he has special time and they all want it, too,' said Mrs. Harriman, who has no household or child-care help."[179]

Yet, it's important to point out that also multiples crave and need alone time with parents. Many parents will on autopilot know to shield their older singleton with some alone-time from time to time, but the need to also do so for each of the multiples is not necessarily apparent. Yet, as Swedish twin and triplet researcher Britta Alin-Åkerman notes, triplets have a different psychological situation than twins, and of course singletons, because they must constantly and to a greater degree compete for the attention, stimulation and love of their mother (parents).[180]

You might be persuaded of the 'why' by now, but still wonder how in the world you'll manage. After all, taking just one child to a cafe at a time might be tricky and you might not want to make a time dent in your own parental happy hour come bedtime by keeping one child up longer (although both ideas have been applied with success by parents of triplets). Therefore, it might be reassuring to hear that I for one would like to raise the flag for the small, regular moments you can incorporate into a day or a week. Fortunately, it's the accumulation of these little things that make up a larger life, and so it's the little things that count.

a) Let them know they can always speak with you in private.

Make it clear that they can speak with you in private. Mariann says that one time "Mum asked you to go away. We were in my room, and I was talking with her about something and then you guys showed up. She told you that she was talking with me and could you please go away. I remember it well because I loved it. She was all mine." Just like Mariann, I treasure memories of time dedicated to just me. I would be in the kitchen, talking with my mother about something, when the door would open, and a sibling would walk in. "Not just yet," my mother would say. "I'm talking with Kari now. Can you please go upstairs and play a bit longer? I'll let you know when you can come down." Time was made just for me and there was a willingness to take that time away from someone else if I needed her.

b) Introduce individual moments into a shared good-night ritual.

As a stroke of genius when the house was expanded (as the family size and noise level increased) my sisters and I had individual rooms spread out as a fan, at 180 degrees. Mariann's was in the middle, walled in by a sister on each side. If Trude and I both leaned forward, we could see each other from our beds. The beauty of the design was that it made it possible for a parent to stand by the entrance of each of our rooms and speak or sing to all of us at the same time. Yet, every night, after a few songs (if it was our mother, or one song if it was our father), whoever put us to bed would come by each room for a hug and a few private words. I would hear the shushed voices from my sisters' rooms while I awaited my turn.

c) Invite one to join in on a chore or bring just one on an errand.

"Kari, do you want to come with me and pick up the mail?" My father will still single out one of us if we're all at home and ask if a specific person will accompany him the fifty meters to the mailbox down the road. And, instead of going, "Who will do the dishes with me?" he adds a name: "Trude, you and I do the dishes really quick now, okay?" Although my father was quick to point out that one-on-ones with the three girls were something they could have done more of when we were little, well, he was doing it—and he still is. While you might not particularly delight in drying the dishes with your father as a child, it makes you feel special to be asked and it gives the two of you time together, alone.

d) Do separate projects with each.

There's another way to give a child the sense that you see them, and that's to pick up on something that interests the child and do it with them. That said, what comes first, an interest by the child or an interest that is picked up on as something specific to the child by others and thus further encouraged in the child?

Some psychologists argue that children find and fill separate niches in a family to get parental attention and approval.[181] Makes perfect sense to me. It might be so easy that there is a small difference in interest, and when that is noticed and encouraged you latch onto it.

If you were to ask my father about our differences as children, as I did, he will point out that we had different interests. "You had more reading, writing, and that thing about horses." Indeed, they made me *me* and allowed me to be seen and noticed on my own.

"That thing about horses" is probably the most outspoken or demonstrative interest I've ever had. I filled my jacket pockets with sugar cubes, I craned my neck to have a good look whenever we drove past a horse, and twice a month when about eight years old, I'd accompany a classmate to a nearby farm to sit on top of a sleepy, old horse for an hour or two. Yet, one of the best things about the horses was that my mother supported me in this interest.

When I asked for riding boots, she suggested I'd save money and that she'd help. Eventually the two of us travelled to the nearby city where I handed over a bag full of coins to get my very own boots and helmet. When I was at the peak of my horse obsession, I also wrote a story, *Christmas in the Stables*, half on paper and half on the thick beige cardstock you find at the back of a notepad (obviously when I ran out of paper), and Mum again saw a possible joint project. "Why don't you turn it into a proper book?" she suggested. "Write it again on proper paper, and I'll help with the illustrations."

Indeed, I loved everything about horses.

Except, well, the actual horses.

I was secretly afraid of them—a tight-lipped secret that almost got out the summer my parents sent their four youngest ones to a weeklong riding camp. My greatest source of stress that week was trying to remain on the black Shetland pony. I cried everything but brave tears the day I was assigned to a million-meter-tall brown horse. Fortunately it was the owner of the stables and not one of my siblings who came to look for me after I didn't turn up when it was time to take the horses out. Bless him; he never told on me but simply shifted the riders around. Still, this was *an idea* I was firmly committed to: I was crazy about horses because that was my *thing*.

So that was me. What about the others? "What did Mariann and Trude have?" I ask my father. "You know what, I can't recall," he replies. That left me thinking, because truthfully neither can I. What I realized is that there was a whole lot of *me* when we were little. When it came to finding separate niches to fill, I excelled at the game. My sisters found overlapping ones, or simply weren't as demonstrative as I was in shouting their obsession and self-definition to the world.

How did Mariann feel about all of this when she was little?

"It's difficult to talk about even today. It's a matter of feelings we might not have spoken that much about. We've shared all, but we haven't really spoken about our roles in childhood and thoughts about attention from parents. It wasn't singularly positive for Trude and

I. But at the same time, it was your thing that I was happy for you to have.

"You say interests, but it wasn't necessarily different interests. We were all happy when we went to the riding camp for a week one summer, but you were the one who got to live out the dream, not because we were so different—because we also wanted to. But it was a bit scary, so maybe that's why we didn't insist on also joining. But I did in fact write in my diary that I was going to use money from my birthday to buy riding boots.

"With books and Mum and things—I also recall that. That as well became a thing between you and Mum. Trude and I didn't interfere in that."

"Didn't Mum find books also for you?" I ask.

As little, I'd stand in our living room, browsing through the bookshelves next to Mum, and she'd say, "Here's one," passing me a book she thought I'd enjoy. I always did, even the ones that were frankly too advanced for me, like *Sophie's Diary*, whose heavily philosophical parts I skimmed to get to the good bits about the adventurous girl. But it was a book that was suggested to *me*.

"No," Mariann says, "she only found books for you. It was you and Mum. And it was your thing, and therefore Trude and I didn't go into it. So we had a lot of respect for each other whenever someone got that attention. Then, in a way, I think Trude and I went a bit away from it. I wasn't that keen on reading and you read so ridiculously much, so compared with you I read little. You of course define yourself in comparison with the others. When it comes to writing, we were also good at that. It was in a way made a bit of artificial divisions there, which then segmented. I don't want to exaggerate things here, but it did feel a bit sore. It's important for parents to make sure they have that individual bond with everyone or create individual projects with all. I didn't necessarily want to read the same books that you did, but I would have liked that attention from Mum."

As my sister points out, your children might not all want to join in on an activity but do try your best as a parent to spend time one on one with each and develop separate activities or projects you can have with each. Help them find a niche—something they can "own," which means they share something with you that's just theirs.

4. Help your children bond with each other by at times letting just two be together.

I'd say it's much the same principle that applies: spending time together—alone. As an example, I have fond memories of a weekend Stig and I spent at our maternal grandparents when we were about eight and ten, which tells a lot, as that weekend was probably also the one I've been scolded the most in my life.

You see, we didn't quite listen when our grandfather told us to shut the front door carefully. Instead we let the wind bang it shut behind us as we ran out to play, eventually fracturing its upper glass pane. My grandfather turned red and my grandmother quickly ushered us down to wait in our assigned bedroom while she calmed down our grandfather. Us two allies in unintended crime, sitting on top of a bed speaking in nervous, hushed voices, is now a memory Stig and I laugh at together. "Do you remember the door at grandpa's?" one of us says with a laugh.

It was a special treat to get to play on your own just with Stig, something I'm certain he knew well, as he'd sometimes stage competitions between the three of us in which the prize was getting to tidy his room with him or receive toys he had outgrown.

Stig says, "As I've told you already, it was fantastic to have three playmates, always someone to play football or cards or monopoly with at the cabin. The other side was that sometimes it wasn't all that with three sisters who got lots of attention, although I don't think it was a big problem, just a little odd at times, like that story of me kicking this lady in the leg as a kid. I don't remember it as a big deal over time, perhaps because I quickly got distracted from those thoughts by our playing. I might have been a bit grumpy because of the three, and then—*activity*!"

The close sibling bond might come at a later stage

A close sibling bond is something all parents wish for their children. While I'm not about to wallpaper over the challenges of being the singleton sibling of multiples, I'm sure many parents will find reassurance in knowing that sibling bonds can grow stronger with the years.

One of the strongest traditions in my family is gathering our entire family at my father's place for Christmas along with a wonky tree and the rain on the Norwegian coast. Over the years spent apart and abroad, it's been the one time of year we've all been able to gather: all five siblings with partners and children. Some years, when my oldest brother Tord is to celebrate with his wife's family in mid-Norway, he'll plead with the rest of us to push Christmas forward a weekend so that he first gets a chance to visit home and celebrate. As he says it, "It's not Christmas without you".

When Tord next connects with me on FaceTime, I ask him what it was like to grow up having triplets as sisters.

"Today, I don't think about the fact that you're triplets. You're my sisters."

"So what was it like when we were children?"

"I'm not going to exaggerate and paint a dark picture. It was okay."

Okay? "What does that mean?" I ask.

"You can interpret it as you want, *ha ha ha.* Joking aside, it was just *fine*. It was like having three, well four, little siblings."

Although my mother once told me they tried to not use Tord for babysitting, he still at times became a third parent in arms, often tasked with keeping us in check when out travelling. When I push Tord for more, asking if he recalls any episodes from when we're little, it's precisely one of the travel-related ones that makes him chuckle.

"I do remember one episode. We were going to Stavanger and drove through all of Karmøy in the Peugeot, with four little brats in the back and me in the middle of you all. Four brats *howling* the entire time, and I'm being told off by Mum and Dad because I'm not able to keep you quiet. I'll never forget that. That's the kind of everyday episode from my childhood."

"But we got better with the years, right?"

"When I moved away from home, it got better."

I laugh, then realize he might actually mean it. He probably does. "Are you serious?" I ask. "Was it *that* hard?"

"*Naaah*," Tord says, "I was just joking with you, but I can't bring it all up. It's part of the past. But to have siblings today, that's *really great*. We can meet up and have a coffee, participate in runs together and do things together. That's nice, right?"

CHAPTER 16

Leaving comparisons behind—leaving to be just me

Hanging around with your co-multiples means comparisons, silently or loudly and whether you like it or not. The many tales of twins choosing to spend large chunks of their adult lives apart have come as no surprise to me: it takes strength to deal with boundless comparisons, and that strength comes with life experience—of having had people see *just you*. Sometimes that's easier to do if you remove one or two factors from the equation—at least for a while.

Some years ago, a journalist came around to my father's for an interview for a parent magazine. The angle? The new family situation many parents experience when their children move abroad—and seemingly never return.

Eight years before that interview, I was in a taxi pulling away from the apartment in Oslo that I'd been sharing with Trude and three others. Now I was off to study in Spain for a year, and looking back at Trude and Mariann waving goodbye, I shed a tear. If I had known it would be over ten years until we'd be living in the same country again, I would have cried a lot harder.

Those years weren't planned, but over time my sisters and I revealed possibilities to each other by every few years shifting countries both in Europe and in the world, and we jointly reduced the motivation for travelling back home. Because why go back to Norway if Mariann and Trude weren't there after all? Yet, the bigger question was perhaps, Why did we three, who spent our early lives so intimately together, feel for such a long time that we needed our very own countries?

In my twenties, I spoke with my then-boyfriend, now husband about my relationship with my sisters. "It sounds bonkers," I said, "but sometimes I think we're so close because we're apart. As adults we've lived each our independent life, in different countries. We don't have to compete or to be compared at all."

"I've often thought about that too," he replied.

Eeeeeveryone's a twin researcher

Nowadays, I rarely tell people that I'm an identical triplet. For starters, one's siblings don't really come up much in conversations between adults, and if they do, I tend to refer to them as "my sisters," partly because saying "I'm a triplet" hijacks a conversation and gives me a sense that everybody by default has me on their bucket list. ("Oh my god, I've never met an identical triplet before! *Ka-ching*! Check!")

Mainly, however, it's because the conversation inevitably veers into comparisons. "Tell me, how similar are you? Can people tell you apart? How are you different? Are you different? Are you the same height? Same weight? Are you best friends? Are the three of you just as close? Would I be able to say if I met your sisters tomorrow instead of you, or would I think it's you?"

Comparisons are how we make sense of this world. Yet, multiples are at the extreme end. As one researcher points out, "Only multiples have the burden of being born together so that every stage of their development can be compared directly with their multiple siblings."[182] Who walked first? Said the first word? Lost the first tooth? Tied those shoes first? You get the idea.

We also hold the key to understanding this world a wee bit better, which is why there is an entire field of study called "twin study," because if you're trying to figure out how nature and nurture interact, multiples are front and center in the debate. To what extent do we become someone because of our genes, and what is the role of our environment?

The coolest twin study to date is arguably the one that may one day help put a man on Mars, featuring American twin astronauts Scott and Mark Kelly. In 2015 Scott went on a one-year spaceflight while Mark stayed on the ground as Scott's control group. With the same genetics but with one in space and another on Earth, it offered a unique chance to examine the effects of long-term space travel on our bodies. Some preliminary results of the study, which is simply called "Twins Study" by NASA,[183] are now in, and among them is longer telomeres, the structure of our genes that's indicative of how old we are, which in turn lead the media to speculate that NASA had found "the fountain of youth." Simply head to space.

Though, as all twins know, there's also another take on that. Here's an excerpt from an interview with the two:

Didn't Scott get a little bit younger because of time dilation? Maybe not because of the telomeres, but something like a couple milliseconds or something like that?

Scott Kelly: Yeah, by like three milliseconds.

Mark Kelly: No, no, Scott. I think if you actually add up your 520 days, because I did this, I saw what people say is that per day, at 17,500 miles an hour, I think where I used to be six minutes older, I think I am now—if you did the math correctly—it's six minutes and 13 milliseconds.[184]

Indeed, there's much to thank twin studies for, and I'm all for the pursuit of knowledge. But, admittedly, I'm not equally thrilled when *I'm* the research subject. In fact, multiples turn everyone into a researcher, says my brother Stig.

"What I find interesting is that people in a way need to categorize you, or maybe that they're fascinated about doing it. 'Yes, you're triplets, but that one is that and that one is that...' In a way, they turn into amateur psychologists and want to analyze and see and find differences, to see if they can manage to find differences in what they in a way expect to be similar."

Because while, at least for identical multiples, it's the sameness that first catches people's interest, it's the differences that have the greatest appeal. Stig explains with another example, his wife. "When we go shopping for Christmas presents for you and I come up with something, I say, 'What do you think of this?', and she'll reply, 'Whom are you thinking of that one for?' If I then go, 'It's for Mariann,' then she'll say, 'No, no, no, that one's more Kari and her personality. Mariann is sportier. So, let's find something sportier for her.' And that's when I point out that you can overlap a bit. It's not like Mariann *only* wants sport clothes, *ha ha ha*, right? I know she is very interested and follows you very closely."

When I showed that passage to Trude, she said: "Mariann was the first one who ran a marathon, but we also worked out lots. But she became 'the sporty one'—why? I was often told I was prettier. I've often felt that you had lots of charisma. I heard that a lot. That Kari was so charismatic. But don't I have that?"

For multiples, who are always seen in reference to just one or two others, comparisons are also about ownership of something. The math's simple: If you're less than, it's not yours to keep. If you're more than, it's all yours. There's only one who can be tallest, funniest, smartest, fastest, thinnest, nicest and any other part of your looks or personality that can be made part of a competition you never really signed up for.

"I think everyone can learn something from the fact that we needed to develop coping mechanisms as children," Mariann says when we speak about this. "You get so much information all the time about who you are. Fortunately, we had many who said many different things. You learn to distinguish a bit that whatever is said is how other people see you. Already from a very young age you need to distance yourself a bit. That's how I use it also today. It's not necessarily who I am. It's more that *you* have seen a small piece of *me*."

That's when Mariann mentioned her year apart from Trude and I as exchange students in different countries at sixteen and seventeen. It was the first time we spent lengthy periods apart. The first month I cried every night. I was due to live with a Costa Rican family for a year, learning Spanish and going to a local "colegio," a secondary school. Half a year later, Trude travelled to the US and Mariann to Guatemala where they too would be living as exchange students.

"I thought it was so fantastic in Guatemala because it was just *me*," Mariann says. "Because I often felt I came in the shadow of you and Trude. It was often like that when we were children. You were the smart one, Trude was the funny one. I had nothing."

She paused. "You had scars, Trude had a mole, and I had nothing."

I started to laugh; Mariann joined in after a second. It was simply too absurd. *The mole, the scar, and the nothing.* (Flip back to chapter nine if you can't quite recall my scars).

Mariann laughingly protested, "But that *is* how it was. 'No, you have nothing, so you must be Mariann!' Every time I have been alone, then it has been a bit good as well. Because then I can be everything. Then I get to be the fun one, the smart one and also myself. Everything I am worth."

The couple's effect: why twins might have a harder time than triplets

One of the challenges multiples face, is that when people ask questions or offer their opinions, we're burdened with the idea that it's polite to answer or at least listen. As a child, I felt obliged to hear people out. I patiently waited until they had seemingly figured me out, until they had proven to me that they could tell us apart. If I took little interest or tried to get out of the situation, it often felt like the wrong was on my side. I failed at properly appreciating how they saw me. And, as a child, you're wary of social sanctions. So I stayed put.

"Well, yes and no," Mariann says of that idea. "I think it also has to do with the fact that you were always left hoping. Would you clock in on all accounts this time? Because people would disagree. Labels changed. Perhaps this round would be more favorable than the last?"

I remember that feeling, which is perhaps why I've always assumed triplets have it easier than twins. I've often thought of the twin world as one that runs on the binary system, while triplets more often end up on a spectrum. Being a trio throws people off the scent. No matter how hard someone tries to pin you down, there is often one category missing and it's also harder to keep track of three people's labels at all times.

I still remember a set of twins I met while at university, simply because so much about them seemed, well, *forced*. It was like they had carefully and deliberately divided the world between them. One was blond whilst the other had died her hair dark. One opted for a bohemian style while the other dressed rather conservatively. One was at the faculty of social sciences and the other studied at the faculty of humanities. Their group of friends didn't overlap at all. I remember thinking, *I couldn't have done that even if I wanted to*, and perhaps because of that, we could be who we were as well, even though that meant being quite similar.

Multiples not only share genes: they also (except for the rare ones adopted to different families) form part of each other's environments. With that we've added a psychological dimension as well as a genetic one to the link between the two (or three). It's what researchers call the "couple's effect."

Coined by French psychologist Rene Zazzo, the "couple's effect" refers to how twins look for niches to establish uniqueness and independence. (Fairly similar to the idea that all children within a family seek to find their own particular niche, see chapter 15). By doing so, they may end up exaggerating differences between each other.

It's the classic game of compare and contrast, converted into a tool to figure out who you are. So one way twins can be recognized as different is to simply join forces in eliminating as much personality overlap as possible. Like the girls I knew at university, if multiples appear to be exact opposites, they may have chosen polarization as a means of establishing their own identities.

Here's a comment by an identical twin in a set that chose different academic paths, "He's studying classics at Oxford and I'm studying natural sciences at Cambridge; I think we're quite conscious of being very different in terms of what we want to do with our lives. Life would be a treadmill of constant comparisons, otherwise."[185]

And, here's another twin comment in the same vein: "Being a twin is a sort of quiet battle to establish your own individual identity, especially when you look as similar as we do. We'd never dream of ordering the same dinner at a restaurant, because that would be weird. We're both very aware of the constant pressure to try to carve out any differences."[186]

It's seemingly a conundrum that when it comes to certain traits, identical twins reared together are less like each other than identical twins brought-up apart.[187] And, just as interesting, there is apparently "some indication", Australian researcher David Hay says, that fraternal twins "may become more similar in personality when they leave home and establish separate lives, since there is no longer the pressure from the other twin."[188]

Twin researcher Alessandra Piontelli's take on Zazzo's theory on this, is: "According to Zazzo the canny similarities in twins reared apart are due to the fact that some genetic traits can only be expressed when the twins are not living together. When they are, the 'couple effect' has the power to mask, attenuate, and counterbalance the powers of heredity."[189]

Nurture may mask nature. The couple effect may dampen genetic factors. No wonder we needed some time apart.

Time apart goes hand in hand with continued, extreme closeness

Many parents of seemingly inseparable multiples worry that they won't be able to let someone else into their lives. Perhaps due to quotes like this from a fellow twin in a Guardian article aptly called, *I've never needed anyone else: life as an identical twin:* "We were so close that I never felt I needed anyone else. All the way through my undergraduate studies, I thought, "Well, I already have the closest friend I'm ever going to find. I don't have any gaps that need filling".

It's also what I was stunned to realize when I began thinking of our closest friends. All of them are friends we each made when we were apart, living in different countries.

In her dead-honest book *One and the Same*, identical twin and American journalist Abigail Pobgrein explores twinship, and much of her book is about trying to accept that her twin sister has been pulling away from her for years.[190] It feels like a zero-sum game, her sister says, stressing that it's not about rejecting her twin; it's about claiming something.

"It's like, if I'm choosing you and I'm spending time with you, then I'm not developing this other side of my life. And my whole life was with you before. So I'm trying to have some other life besides you."[191]

Pobgrein objects to her sister's boundaries and turns to psychologist Joan A. Friedman to decode the dynamic between the two. She says she's almost scolded by Friedman, who says her sister "simply wants to have her own sense of self" and that she is to recognize that her sister needs space. And here's the key bit, "not because she's upset or resentful", Friedman replies, "but so she can grow apart from you, which will ultimately enable her to be close to you."[192]

I believe that's the gist of it. *It's growing fully apart so you're able to be close.*

And sometimes, a bit (or a lot) of geographical distance is what's needed to bring us there.

You see, I'm drawn to my sisters.

Just recently I had a phone call with Mariann, and as we were about to hang up I said, "Talk to you next week!" She laughed. We both did. "Tomorrow!" I hurried to say, as I had obviously misspoken.

"*Ha ha ha.* Talk to you next week then!"

But when we lived in different countries, days and even weeks could easily pass without talking on the phone. The magnetism weakened, and I went about my life, meeting new people, *needing* other people. That was indeed the reality for most of the ten years I spent abroad before moving back to Norway at 31.

Yet, even during these years, when I lived in Spain, Latvia and Belgium, I tried to figure out how to spend as much time with them as I possibly could. For six months during our twenties, Mariann and I overlapped in Belgium: I was working in Brussels while she studied in the nearby city of Bruges. I would leave work at six in the evening, hurry down to the train station, and be at Mariann's at eight, which was just enough time for a little catch-up in person before I spent the night on a mattress in her dorm room and took the train back in the early morning before work.

Years later, after Mariann had ticked off long-term stays in Morocco, Norway, Malaysia, and then Norway again, Trude was the one who moved in next door after years in Australia, the U.K., Hungary, and Norway. Or, she moved to the neighboring country, the Hague in the Netherlands. But this new situation of merely a few hours on a train seemed like a breeze compared with having to catch expensive flights.

While in the Hague and Brussels, Trude and I travelled to see each other like Mariann and I had once done. Hurrying out from work in the late afternoon to catch a three-hour train that would give us an hour or two together in the evening before getting up early in the morning to make it back to work in the neighboring country. When Trude eventually moved to Norway, I cried on the journey back from the Hague to Brussels. "Who knows when we'll have this again?" I said, trying to explain it to my then-boyfriend, now husband.

I know now. It's been several years since that conversation, but my husband and I now have a house just outside of Oslo, within walking distance of Trude and driving distance of Mariann. Today, my closeness with my sisters, both geographically and emotionally, is a conscious choice. We've had the breathing space to become fully secure in ourselves, and when people compare, when we ourselves compare, I know all three of us can cope with that. Because people have seen each of us. Just the one.

And, to those parents out there who worry about the impact on the twin bond by spending so much time apart, I'd say it's what remained the backbone throughout my years abroad. As another twin nicely put it, "Even though we've spent many years apart, she's always been the still point in the turning world for me. That will never change."[193]

Downplay comparisons: what can you do as a parent?

1. Be protective of your children when people approach to comment.

When family members, friends, or even a stranger asks you who's the more outgoing or sporty or if they're all equally outgoing, that's your cue to change topic. Opt for a pleasantry on how they're all wonderful in their own ways and deflect with a question of your own. If pushed, be frank in response. Say how it's a good, general rule of thumb not to compare children, and especially not multiples who are measured against each other more than other siblings. Yes, this might come off as rude, but, truthfully, so is asking you, often in front of your children, to judge who possesses what trait. No one would feel comfortable examining their seven-year-old and nine-year-old in detail out loud while said children listen in, so why should someone do that to your multiples?

2. Don't be the one exaggerating differences.

We all try to fulfil our perceived roles, and we understand our place in the world through the expectations we are met with.

Parents' beliefs about their children, and the comparisons they make, may cause differences to be magnified.[194] Just like with Trude's mole, you should be aware of whether you're making something big out of something small and telling the entire world, including your child, to notice it. And, keep in mind "the couple's effect". Maybe they're both funny and maybe all three in reality could be equally outgoing, there's just not space for them all to be it at the same time?

3. Don't compare, describe.

If someone's the "sporty one," the position as Sporty Spice is taken. "Being sporty" makes it possible for all two or three to aspire to the role. To paraphrase Mariann, let them be all of it.

4. Talk with them about their feelings about being a multiple and comparisons.

Let your children talk openly with you about their feelings for each other, how it is to be together, and how they feel about being compared with each other. Ask them open questions, obviously when you're alone with one, and let your child reply.

When your children seem old enough for this kind of talk, help them realize that categories can be fluid and that they can all be sporty, funny, smart etc. If you're one for props, some cutlery will do the trick. A knife, a spoon, a fork, a spork (fork and spoon), and a piece of travel cutlery that combines spoon, fork and knife. Show them to your children and explain how they can also be many similar things. They can all be nice, smart, fun, and whatever else they feel and see in themselves. A knife is no less of a knife even though travel cutlery exists.

CHAPTER 17

Romantic relationships for multiples: the truth

I once read a comment by a triplet mother, who after skimming a book on twins felt scared, she said, as it seemed like no twins were able to grow close to their partners. Their twinship somehow put their romantic relationship in the background. Indeed, twins might not be straight-forward soulmates, but trust me, our bond is not marriage kryptonite. On the contrary, a shared silver medal between a spouse and one's co-twins might be gold-glittered.

One line stayed with me longer than the guy who said it. It happened in my early twenties during a conversation with a former, almost forgotten boyfriend.

"I hope that one day you will want to call me first."

He'd said it after I'd received happy news and had called to tell him. I was midway through my story when he interrupted, saying, "Have you already told Mariann and Trude?"

I genuinely wish I could say I replied something reassuring, something demonstrating that I had picked up on the fact that he simply wanted to be closer—closest, the one. But no. Instead I blurted out, "Of course!"

He didn't reply.

"Why do you ask?"

That's when he gave me his line.

Truth be told, there was no flattery in it, as far as I was concerned. I was way too busy thinking, *What the hell? Did he just make my call about him? Had my wonderful news been turned into a petty competition between him and my sisters?* My second thought was, *Don't be ridiculous.* As far as I was concerned, there was no competition.

I know, I know. I've grown up since and have learned to be more sympathetic to the fact that that being number one is everyone's priority in a relationship.

Let's admit it: a twin is not a straight-forward soulmate

I'm sure for most people it seems like a clear line of logic. Find your soulmate; one asks, the other nods; start of shared story. Yet, in writing this book, I've come across numerous accounts by twins of how the twinship takes precedence—their twin simply comes first. It's a fact their life partner, if there is one, will simply have to accept. As one husband, who'd been married to a twin for fifty years, said, "Let me put it to you this way: God forbid I had to stand on a cliff with my wife and her twin, and make a decision which one of us was going to be pushed, I might as well jump."[195]

As simple as that.

Unfortunately, it's not that simple.

Most people find it tremendously hard to accept that despite having found their "one," there's this nagging sense that their soulmate might be closer with someone else. There are those who will argue that this smacks of febrile optimism in a world beset with divorce, but relationships, both when it comes to how long they last and how satisfied people are to be in them, have been shown to be positively associated with the belief in soulmates.[196,197] The snag, however, is that it's largely only in cases where people consider their partner to be their *matching* soulmate.[198]

And, I'm afraid that when it comes down to the art of loving properly, twins seem to be failing. In a study of adult twins, many spoke openly of how difficult it can be for a husband or wife to accept the emotional bond their spouse shares with their twin.[199] To illustrate, here's the fairly straightforward user 'Twinhell', who I found typing angrily in an Internet forum with other unhappy twin spouses:

"If you are considering a relationship with a twin, start running, run till you can't run anymore and never look back. If you are in a marriage with a twin, get out. Marriage is difficult enough without dealing with the twin bond, and life is too short to live that way, as a tag-along. There are about 5 billion people on this planet, surely there is someone for you that is NOT a twin."[200]

Ouch.

As I scrolled and scrolled and scrolled, I felt like crossing my arms defensively over my chest. I can't really recap quickly (as my husband said when I sent him the link, "My God, there are hundreds of them?!"), so instead here are a selected few replies to the post "Am married to a twin."[201]

- "How sad is it though, when the person you love the most doesn't love you the most."

- "Deep down, a lot of the time I feel the twin comes first which is difficult to accept."
- "The twin can do no wrong. No matter how big a self-esteem you have, you will feel insecure as second best to their twin."

I would be in full denial if I didn't admit that I get what these spouses are talking about, but they don't have the full story. For starters, happy spouses of twins don't take to Internet forums with usernames like "Twinhell". That's obviously bad news for those of us who run the risk of potential partners googling what they've supposedly gotten themselves into. As one potential twin spouse put it, "I'm trying to accept the same thing [the twin bond] and I'm not even married yet, trying to figure out if this is a bad idea."

Take it from me: It's not. There's just very little out there for soothing your nerves. But what you, and other twin partners need, is for us multiples to refrain from pulling our twin or triplet trump card, even if our hand might be twitching to do so. Not quite following? Let me explain with the help of my own romantic relationship.

The night it dawned on me: a couple is one-plus-one
A while back I asked my husband if it had ever been an issue for him that I was an identical triplet. "It's never really been an issue. I always just saw you," he replied. And, as if reading my mind (the one writing this book and mining for material), he added, "No offence."

I suppose it was the perfect answer, and yet I felt immensely disappointed. Honestly, a little irrational part of me wanted him to see it as a major sticking point.

Because it was for me.

And, so, to the story of my boyfriend's proposal.

I wasn't prepared for it. Although my friend was holding up her Mojito for a toast, I sat down my own drink.

She'd just let slip that my boyfriend was going to propose.

"I actually thought he would do so this summer," she said. "He got a ring and everything."

My boyfriend and I had just returned from summer holidays in Norway, and I'd met up with a close friend, a girl married to one of his best friends.

"What?" *Now* I took a big sip of my Mojito.

She made me promise not to tell anyone. "He already thinks I've got a big mouth!"

We laughed, and I promised. (I only told Trude and Mariann.)

I headed home to our apartment. I was on my own for the weekend, as my boyfriend was travelling. That Friday night I kept myself in check. Saturday too. But come Sunday I decided to start tidying. *Meticulously.* And there, on top of the wardrobe in the bedroom, in a large black box containing his skiing clothes, inside the pocket of a ski jacket, sat a much smaller blue box.

I know, I know. Not my finest moment. But he should be glad I knew about the proposal beforehand and that I Marie Kondo-ed our place that day to verify the rumor. I've never told him this, as I know it will ruin his magic memory of how the proposal went down—supposedly out of the blue.

"You really had no idea?" he likes to ask me when we reminisce.

"No," I've always answered.

Truth be told, he would look at me more gently if he understood that me knowing was the only reason I agreed immediately to marry him when he asked.

When I opened the box, I sat staring at the ring for a long time. I didn't try it on; that would be taking it too far. (Yes, I'm lying. Of course I tried it on. I just wish I could tell this story in a way that doesn't put me in such a bad light.) I laughed in joy and shed a few tears.

Then, that night, I lay in bed and cried again but not joyfully. It had hit me: the coming question was much bigger than what I'd originally assumed. It wasn't just about whom I wanted to spend my life with, but also whether saying yes to him meant saying no to my sisters. After years of also living abroad, my sisters were back in Norway. They often called me in the morning, when they'd met up at a coffee bar for a quick chat before heading to work, and I found these conversations bittersweet. I'd be walking alone on the sidewalks of Brussels while they were sitting shoulder to shoulder at a cafe in Oslo. At one point, one had probably said, "Hey, why don't we call Kari?" After hanging up, they got to share a hug before starting their work day. I wanted that.

Yet, for the half-French, half-English man I'd fallen in love with, Norway wouldn't necessarily be the dream. For my sisters and I, however, Norway was indeed the dream: we had a running joke about our joint future: "We'll have three houses right next to each other." It was a phrase borrowed from the title of a Norwegian children's TV show we watched when little, with two families almost merging due to the close proximity of their houses ('To hus tett i tett').

Such was the dream that when my boyfriend first met Trude, the first thing she asked was, "Can you live in Norway?" (*I* hadn't even asked him that.)

He'd told my sister yes, but I knew that he, like most foreigners, thought of Norway as a cold, expensive country on the periphery of Europe with its own peculiar language. We were three years into our relationship and tip-toeing around the conversation of what's next. When people asked us, we said, "We'll go to London. Or Oslo." Then shrug. At that moment, it was hard to picture our houses all in a row if I'd agreed to marry him.

I recall thinking, *He can't ask me. Not yet. Am I ready for this, to choose him over them?*

I wouldn't want to face that challenge on the cliff, having to decide whom to save and whom to sacrifice. But I had a simple yet difficult realization that night. If I were to say "yes" to spend my life with him, I would need to own up to the fact that he asked me that question with a rightful expectation that he would have a say in our shared life. It's what one of the unhappy twin spouses online said: "I think twins could stand to learn they are united with another person when they're married and learn to put that person first (or at least SHARE first place)".[202]

I know how ludicrous this must sound, but for me, this was an unprecedented thought: I would need to refrain from using the triplet card, the one where I'd demand that my twinship take precedence, the one that that would make him not first, nor second, not even third in my life, but fourth—tucked well behind my sisters and myself. It dawned on me how narcissistic it would be to tell the love of my life that he should be content as the fifth wheel. Because, if someone chooses you, shouldn't you choose them back? And if those were indeed the rules of the game, who would even choose you?

At our wedding several years later, Trude held a speech my husband didn't quite get, but which made all the sense in the world to me.

Speaking about it today, she says: "The gist of my speech was that I accepted that he now became your best friend and that I thought it was nice—for the first time ever—that someone else was that person for you, because it was really the two of you! I felt wistful, but I was also really proud of myself for being so generous and giving you away." She laughs. "I practiced that speech many times because I just kept on crying. I was insanely touched because I realized that he was so good for you that I was willing to be behind him in your life. Now, that's love!"

Despite her laughter, Trude wasn't too far off the mark. (I'm almost hesitant to write this, as I feel like I'm adding to the piles of weird twin case studies). Way before the wedding, way even before the proposal, I told her I found it challenging to get serious with someone who might never want to live in the same country as her and Mariann. "Nonsense," she replied. "You're going to be with him, Kari. You're going to live in England, and you'll be incredibly happy."

It was the little nudge and confirmation I needed. It was okay to choose someone else.

The hard truth: multiples will hold partners to nearly impossible standards

I'm afraid, however, that for a multiple to find someone we'd like to choose over our co-multiple(s) is a tricky affair. Just like everyone else, you see, we are prone to believe in the soulmate hype. Which is of course a double-bummer; soulmates, per se, are hard to come by, and soulmates that match the standard multiples are used to are even harder to find.

As American psychologist and prominent twin expert Barbara Klein, herself an identical twin, puts it in a compact one-liner, "Twins expect more from other people and have to learn to live with less."[203] In Klein's research of adult twins, both identical and fraternal twins said their twinship created relationship challenges. And the main culprit? What she and other researchers call 'twin yearning'.[204] When I first read about it, I thought it sounded bonkers. Apparently, twins try to re-create twin-like relationship with others, so we can enjoy the same emotional and intellectual intensity we're used to.[205] Yet, at second thought, it sounded perfectly reasonable. Because what do you do if you've already enjoyed an incredibly close and intense relationship all your life and then go out into a world largely populated by non-twins looking for your big love? You try to make twins out of people. The obvious downside is that the type of relationship multiples long for with others is extremely difficult or nearly impossible to replicate with other people whom we're close to.

In her book on twin and triplet psychology, British researcher Audrey C. Sandbank, notes the same: "Twins, who for many years have lived with someone who understood their moods and feelings and who may have intuitively known what they were thinking or what they would like to do, may feel disappointed and cheated if their new partner fails to live up to such standards."[206]

"Do you think I've made you into my twin?" I ask my husband after telling him about this research, to which he matter-of-factly replies, "Yeah I think probably you have."

He then hesitates.

"I wouldn't necessarily say made me into your *twin*. I would say we have a very, very close relationship, which I think is a good thing, but I wouldn't say it's you making me into your twin. I'd say it's coincidental that that is the relationship I would like to have too. Whether it's by chance or luck, we don't know."

I don't agree and tell him that.

"When we got together you didn't share as much as you do now."

"That's true as well. Again, I wouldn't say you made me into your twin, but I would say that you have expected a level of closeness and openness, which is perhaps something I wasn't good at the beginning of our relationship and which has developed over time. Whether that has been deliberate by you or not, I don't know. But when I compare us with other people, it is true that we are extremely close, and we do a lot of things together, but I like that."

"So how close are we?"

He grins, and his reply makes me laugh. "Twinesque."

Wait, there are more challenges for partners of multiples

Researchers say the intensity in a relationship that twins are after might baffle others. I get that. It's suddenly being in a relationship with someone who ever since they were little have had such a high degree of intimacy with one or two others and that you're to match—but it might not be natural for you to do so.

Like Trude says, "It's a bit unfair to the partner. We have known each other all our lives. They should get some slack and be allowed to catch up. I thought about it when my boyfriend suddenly told me, 'Trude, you don't have any filter.' I'm a very open person but I should think a bit about what I expect from others. I forget that others might have a higher threshold for that kind of intimacy. I'm used to having the kind of secureness where I can be entirely open and speak about things that many might even be hesitant to admit to themselves. Because that's the thing, you dare to open up—because the one you tell it to won't ever leave you, the person will understand and even if she doesn't, she will be supportive."

Several twin spouses online said the twin took advantage of their spouse. In their minds their spouse went to too-great lengths to help.

Yes. In many ways, they're right. Yet, 'taking advantage of' implies unfairness and that's where these spouses and I part ways. It comes down to having someone's back. As a spouse, you look out for your partner; your partner has yours, but also looks out for their twin.

In our mid-twenties, one of us was introduced to the office by the new boss as someone who'd never have a sick day: if she was ill, surely one of her identical triplet sisters would step in and they'd be none the wiser. Everyone laughed, but little did they know that he was pretty spot on. The other two wouldn't necessarily show up in person, but the new colleague was a one-plus-two package deal—two external consultants conjured up via email at a moment's panicked notice.

Having two people around whose instinctive reply is always "yes" is of course reassuring, but it might also breed insecurity. Why just rely on yourself when you can so easily bring in two others to help? Three brains are better than one, after all.

As Mariann put it, "It's a bit 'for better or worse' in the way that we may at times take it for granted that the others will help. I don't have the same expectations of our brothers. I think it comes down to the degree of closeness. As an example, you feel more overwhelmed with gratitude if a friend takes the day off to help you pack up an apartment than if your boyfriend does, as there's more of an expectation of them to help out. So if you add another hundred percent on that one, then you have us."

Now, on the positive side of things, we're looking at the benefits of a close-knit family. Emotional support, practical support. However, I don't need a psychologist (or a frustrated twin spouse) telling me that we're also looking at a lack of boundaries, in that by always saying "yes" you're not protecting yourself. That's because you're not: you'll stretch yourself to the limit to protect *them*. Yet, for this support system to work, it's essential that each multiple places boundaries on themselves. In a world where you know your co-multiples will be there when you ask, hail or sunshine, own deadlines or not, it's also on you to protect them. Sometimes, the right thing to do is to *not* ask for help, because the ones you ask might not have the Just Say No-card at hand.

Although I'm all for openness in relationships, I'd nonetheless caution any partners reading this against sticking your neck out and into a conversation about this particular support system, no matter how draining you believe it might be for your spouse. I'm pretty confident you'll be better off passing them this chapter or slipping one or more copies of twin expert Joan A. Friedman's books onto your spouse's night stand. I suggest you start them off with the aptly titled *The Same but Different: How Twins Can Live, Love, and Learn to Be Individuals*.

Here's Trude again, just in time to help me stress this point: "Today, I sat there watching Mariann and I thought of how much we resemble each other. We are of course very different, but I do feel that you're part of me—I feel so close to you that you become a part of me. That sounds really stupid, so you can't write that. [Sorry, Trude] But it is because we've been treated as one person throughout the years by so many. So, for example, anything negative that goes on you comes back to me. And as little I couldn't separate between me and you as persons. So, if you did anything wrong, then it reflected on me, ergo I had to support you. The threshold for allowing anyone to say anything negative about you is incredibly low, because I take it personally. I know I haven't managed to establish a good boundary there. I'm aware of that, *ha ha ha*. But I feel that I'm perfectly comfortable with that too!"

No, twins dating twins wouldn't be easier

Some twins simply give up; they opt for dating other twins. It's not a joke: there are online dating sites exclusively for twins. As the creators of one such site put it: "Have you run into difficulties with your partner not understanding your twin relationship? Never again if you're dating another twin!"[207] Whatever you think about it—and I speak as someone who once dated a twin—I'd caution against it. It's doubly difficult.

It is also brilliant. Why?

Above all, other multiples are relaxing people to be around. If you're a multiple dating another multiple, you don't have to go through all the questions. There's nothing intriguing, there's nothing new, and there's no need to explain anything. It just is—on both sides. At least *after* you discover it is on both sides. Here's a conversation from the first date with the identical twin who went on to be my boyfriend for a while:

"I'm an identical twin," he said as we ping-ponged first date questions.

"Really?" I replied, but before I could say anything else, he ran with it. On and on about the twin magic. All I could do was to sit back and wait for him to run out of breath or anecdotes and volley the question back to my side of the court.

"So… do you have any sisters or brothers?"

"Yes, I have two older brothers."

I admit it: I paused for dramatic effect. "Oh, and I am an identical triplet."

According to his twin brother, that's the stupidest he has ever felt on a date.

Other multiples also know better than comparing a partner to their siblings. When multiples date multiples, there's no one around to say things like the following, all examples from my past dating experiences:

- "Your sister has a different upper lip than you."
  (Indeed, it's fuller, thanks for noticing).

- "I almost kissed Mariann when she walked in the door. I thought it was you!" (Why tell me that?)
- "I could have been with Mariann, but not with Trude." (Good to know we're not all just the same.) When I shared this romantic nugget with my sisters, Mariann went, "*What*, like I would ever be with him?" while Trude said, "*What*?! *Ha ha ha*, why not me?!" before adding, "He couldn't be with me either?! *Ha ha ha*," as Mariann once had a similar conversation with her now-ex. As always, remove the twin context and it becomes apparent that telling your girlfriend, "Uhm, I could probably have dated your younger sister, but not your older one" means showing yourself the door.

When I first met the identical twin of my then-boyfriend, I immediately liked him. Obviously, I didn't get all their inside jokes, but I did get that they had a bond that made my boyfriend a happier and more secure person, just like I had with my sisters. Why in the world should any of us feel threatened by that? He and I had been together less than half a year at the time, whilst we had twenty-something years' worth of memories with our respective co-twin and co-triplets. We were both the new addition and growing close to someone takes time.

It comes down to respecting that bond and being aware that this other person is a constant in their life. It's what Trude replied when I asked her how important I am in her life: "You're my person. You're my go-to-person, no matter what it is, then it's you. Now I have a partner that I love, but I've had other relationships with ups and downs. But, you're constant no matter what happens. There is no break-up or divorce when it comes to our relationship".

Now I'm reluctant to continue and tell you the bad news, as I know Twinhell is prone to yell, "I told you so!" But you know what they say about assumptions? Right, it's the mother of all fuck-ups. One day it dawned on me what so many partners of twins discover: the twinship demands precedence. In this case on *both* sides.

"What color do you want on your roof?" the twin, my then-boyfriend, asked me once.

The question came out of the blue, at least for me. He is Danish and was back in Copenhagen for his studies, and I was visiting while on my way to Belgium where I was to start a traineeship. I was 22 and the future was bright, happy, and something best planned a few months at a time. There we were, on our way up this little hill (there are only little hills in pancake-flat Denmark) when he asked about the roof. Indeed, a bizarre question. Yet, it makes sense in Denmark—and *only* in Denmark, where all houses seem to be made of brick, leaving house owners a choice of black or orange roof tiles.

I didn't reply. While I was only softly pedaling on the bicycle to reach the hilltop, my mind was spinning hard. I was suddenly staring my previous denial flat in the face: *his* dream was *my* dream. I dreamed of living next door to my sisters, of being able to pop by in the morning to borrow milk, of saying a quick "hi" after work, and of long summer evenings together on one of our balconies. In my mind my stay abroad was temporary; eventually, in a year or a few, we'd all be back together. Just like he assumed he'd be, here on the outskirts of

Copenhagen, in the same municipality where his brother lived, mere biking distance apart.

(For the sake of this argument and because I'm curious, I just Facebook-stalked my Danish twin ex. His most recent post? Photos of architect sketches for a two-family house he and his twin and their families are having built in Copenhagen. I have no idea what color roof tiles they're going for, unfortunately.)

Finally, some good news: a shared silver can be gold-dusted. Hurrah!

If you're a partner of a multiple reading this, I need you to do the following: close the lid on the standard narrative of what constitutes the one, true love. I promise, doing so is more exciting than it sounds. Because what I need to get across to you, is that a shared gold medal or a close silver doesn't necessarily say anything about the quality of your relationship as compared with other people's relationships,' even though other people in relationships might both firmly tick each other off as *numero uno*.

To persuade you of this, here is a recent conversation I had with Mariann:

"Are you closest with Trude and I or with your husband?"

"In one way I'd say you, because you've known me from childhood and know everything, and we've been through so much together. But the last years we've all lived pretty much apart, and we've all had our very own experiences. But he's is there with me every day, right? You don't know all the details anymore, like if I've had a frustration at work or if something has happened. You do get a closer relationship with the one you're spending most of your day with. But if I were to be asked who I love the most?"

She paused to laugh. I laughed too. Then she continued.

"Then it's not so easy to answer, right? It's a bit like children who end up with divorced parents. You're not supposed to have to choose between your mum and dad."

It's what one of my friends also pointed out one day. I had just entertained him with some comments by twin spouses online when he asked me what my husband thought of my closeness with my sisters.

"Truth be told," I replied, "he says he's never thought about it. And honestly, I think he sees the benefits as well. There have been times when he has replied, 'Why don't you ask one of your sisters instead? They might know better,' so it's probably useful to not be the only sounding board around. I can talk to him about everything, but my sisters can at times relate in a different way, be it because of our shared childhood or gender."

"But I think that's it," my friend said. "He doesn't mind because you two have a very close relationship. I think it comes down to the degree of distance between the closeness in the romantic relationship and the one between the multiples."

He then pointed out that if you yourself long for an intimate connection and feel that you don't have that in your current relationship, then it might be sore to see that your respective other has someone else that she or he can turn to with their innermost feelings. He then made the connection to the idea of soulmates (see, it's a dream that runs deep through all of us). Speaking of his new girlfriend, he said, "We sometimes laugh and say that I'm a male her and she's a female me. We're just the same and like to do the same things. I can be entirely open with her. I never thought I'd have that."

Indeed, remove the romance, attraction, and sex bits and the ideal of a soulmate is pretty much twin mysticism in a different wrapping. Children dream of having a twin, and then they grow up and dream of having a soulmate. It's the two halves of one whole: the other that makes you complete, that is just like you, the profound, life-long intimate connection.

My take on this and the message to partners of multiples is therefore the following: If you're put on the same level as your partner's co-multiples, or he or she find themselves struggling with answering the question of whom they're closest to, that simply means that your romantic relationship is elevated to the same status as that of the Holy Grail of Twinship. One in which you've removed the sibling squabbling and upped it with romance and attraction, which in my book is the closest anyone can come to magic, no matter where you're ranked. And if still in doubt about your status as a matching soulmate, there's thankfully a belief more widely held.

It's this: Love conquers all.

CHAPTER 18

Copacabana grandmas

This is my last chapter, where I tell you that being a multiple is my life's jackpot but also remind you that it's not the full story.

There's an old mantra that says you are born into this world alone and you leave it alone. Well, that's not quite true for all of us. My sisters and I came into this world together, and as children we also assumed we'd leave it together (though obviously, two and four minutes apart). That's how the world works when you're little: it's fair. I would go first, followed by Mariann and then Trude.

Still, it didn't seem all that fair to have to live on without them, so as somewhat morbid little children, we figured a suicide pact, or rather a strenuous hike, was the way to go. When the time came, we would walk to the "Pulpit Rock" and jump off together. If you're not from Norway and haven't watched the nerve-wracking cliff scene in the sixth 'Mission: Impossible', let me briefly explain this place: it's a flat rock face dropping 600 meters into a fjord far below. It is also a demanding several-hour hike to get there. Thinking of it now, if we ever managed to pull ourselves up there as old grannies, it would be time for high-fives all around before we trotted down again.

The horror version society seems to have of twins are the ones who end up together, the ones who find it too hard to be apart, so they end up in a shared home, the Selma and Patty Simpsons out there, the ones who say they "didn't get married because we wanted to stay together," that they were "too busy being twins."[208]

Those are actual quotes. Jessie Baker, a British twin, made the paper with her sister Joan when they decided it was about time to live by themselves in two flats five minutes away from each other—after 96 years together.

As children, this fraternal duo known as "the twins" was made to wear the same clothes, down to the same underwear, and do everything together. Well into their nineties, they still enjoy identical meals and buy the exact same things, whether jumpers or jam, and make sure their hair is styled exactly the same way. In the article Jessie says, 'We love being as identical as we can be."[209]

My first thought when I read the article, was this: See, you can f—them up even if they're not identical. It's what most parents of multiples dread. That if you don't do it right, your duo or trio will end up back where they started. Together. Obviously, it's best to steer clear of raising children who might have a full-on nervous breakdown if their shopping basket deviates from their twin's, who hang on to each other because they've opted out of spending their lives with anyone else, and who feel like their happiness hinges upon the presence of the other at all times.

But my second thought was *Why in the world not?*, because what we need to do when we hear stories of knitting twin grannies sharing a place is to pour everyone a cup of tea and travel six decades back in time, all the way to the proper historic context of women being confined to housekeeping drudgery. Then come join me for a recent conversation I had with my grandmother. It's been twenty years since her husband passed, years that she's filled with travels around Europe with her girlfriends, fulfilling a dream of a driver's license and finally having everything the way she needed to feel true happiness. As my grandmother hung up the phone after a conversation with a male friend, I brightly asked if there was a new man in her life. "*Oh, no no no,*" she protested hard, though with a laugh. "I've had one. I've done mine."

We don't necessarily have to read articles about grannies in matching wool sweaters as *sad* stories. We get to swap the exclamations of "*Ooof!*" as we read for "*Awww,*" because if you remove the bits about being unable to make decisions on your own and at times ending up with meals you dislike because you put a higher premium on having the same than what *you* like, well, then we're left with quotes like these:

Jessie says, "We've always liked being together."

Joan says, "But Jessie is the best sister I could ask for—she's lively, funny and she's always there when I feel down."[210]

Admittedly, I'm trying hard to spin this story. The reason why is that it's my imaginary future we're talking about here. I don't want you to look oddly at me when I stroll down the street arm in arm in arm with Mariann and Trude as cheerful

96-year-olds—as I picture Jessie and Joan do. With a few small tweaks, this whole thing makes for an amazing, enjoyable life time. *Together, apart, together. Ending where we began.*

Whenever I'm in a card shop, I look for the ones with three old women together. It doesn't matter if they look alike or not, I just need three of them. "The Copacabana Grandmas." It's our running joke. It's society's vision of weird twins who live together as adults, yet with bikinis, coconut cocktails and beach parasols. These Rio de Janeiro grannies sprang to life in our university years when my sisters and I were scattered across Europe, moving to a new country every year or so for studies or traineeships. I guess it was a way to high-five our together-ness while spending long periods apart and, joke or not, the idea probably felt reassuring, that while some waiting would be involved, we'd eventually be together again.

Apparently, the close social bonds between twins mean we live longer than most.[211] An American study, which looked at nearly 3000 Danish pairs of same-sex twins, found that identi-cals lived longer than fraternals, who again lived longer than singletons. As one of the study authors put it: "There is benefit to having someone who is socially close to you who is looking out for you."[212]

Indeed, ask me today about being a triplet, and I'll tell you I've won life's jackpot. I once had coffee with a triplet mother who I met in a Facebook group for parents of multiples. Trude came along, and as we sat there talking, the mother got teary-eyed. She laughed and brushed away a tear, "it's like seeing my girls in the future. You look at each other with so much love and tenderness. I really hope they will have it like that." We answered just like Jessie and Joan did: "Yeah, we like spending time together."

Which is true, but the challenge with the story of Jessie and Joan, the Copacabana Grandmas and this entire chapter until now, is that it's simply fodder for the twin fantasy.

One of my aims with this book has been to nuance that picture, which is why I can't end the chapter and this book just yet. I owe that to Madge, the nearly four-year-old (in 1952) that we met in chapter seven, having this conversation with her sister:

Mary to Madge: "Madge, you're a twin."

Madge: "No I'm not, I'm Madge."[213]

Thanks for the reminder, Madge.

Because to have a full life as a full person, you can't first and foremost be a twin or a triplet. I can't be me if I'm always also them and haven't had a chance to be on my own.

Some twins are not ready to do that until their nineties. I'm thankful I came to that realization sooner. Now I have the rest of my life to be just myself—with my sisters close by.

Goodbye and acknowledgements

I just want to say a massive thank you for reading my book, for buying it or lending it from a friend, for passing it on to a friend, a teacher or a neighbor, and for enjoying it (hopefully!).

It means the world to me that this book might make life for lots and lots of young twins and triplets a whole lot easier, and that it may give some comfort, reassurance and guidance to parents of multiples. I don't quite have the words to say how grateful I am, but if you have also reviewed my book on Amazon (please do!), I will raise a glass!

This book would not have happened were it not for the willingness of my family to open up and share. Thank you, a million, to Mariann and Trude – as I told you once; in many ways, this entire book is a love letter to you. To Dad – you are my superhero. To Mum – nothing makes me happier than thinking that this book might be for others what you would have appreciated reading before having us.

Thank you as well to the lovely crowd in the Facebook group 'Parents of identical triplets'. Editors say an author should picture a reader while writing – that's been you guys for me.

And, when my family would have rather read gardening books than yet another draft, the brilliant Chris Ryan came in as the best editor I could dream of. Claire Gillman swooped in after, providing invaluable advice on how to further improve the book.

An immense thank you also to Joan A. Friedman, for your relentless efforts to make this world a better place for twins and triplets. You were the twin expert I nodded along to while drafting this book, leaving me in turn properly starstruck and overjoyed when you said "yes, yes and yes!" to writing this book's foreword and called me your "psychological soulmate".

And, to my husband: I know how lucky I am.

Love, Kari

Copyright

Further reading

Your national multiple birth association
Your first stop as a parent or parent-to-be of twins, triplets or quads should be the website of your national multiple birth association where you should look up your local chapter. Then, when you've secured yourself a support system of fellow super parents who you might meet for a coffee, give a call or a hug, go back to reading the wealth of information normally gathered on these organizations' websites.

"Emotionally Healthy Twins: A New Philosophy for Parenting Two Unique Children," Joan A. Friedman.
As an identical twin, a psychologist specialized in twins, and a mother of five including fraternal twins, Friedman is the ultimate tour guide to the ins and outs of twin psychology. Necessary, thought-provoking and comforting.

"The Same but Different: How Twins Can Live, Love, and Learn to Be Individuals," Joan A. Friedman.
Look up this book's Amazon page and be dazzled by five-star reviews left by adult twins. Few books have readers leaving comments like this: "This book has changed my life."

"Twins in Session: Case Histories in Treating Twinship Issues," Joan A. Friedman.
Although a manual for psychotherapists and educators treating twins, this book has also been warmly embraced by adult twins and twin parents. My favorite Amazon review of this book simply said, "thanks Joan, you're a rock star!"

"Alone in the Mirror: Twins in Therapy," Barbara Klein.
In this gem of a book, Klein, herself an identical twin and psychologist specialized in twins, points out, "it is a twin's fate to have to deal with a double identity". And while glimpses of your other half are hard to shake off, this eye-opening book shows how a twin's path to individuality – to being only one in that metaphorical mirror – can be made significantly less bumpy.

"Twinsight: A Guide to Raising Emotionally Healthy Twins with Advice from the Experts (Academics) and the REAL Experts (Twins)," Dara Lovitz.
When reading this sparkly book, I kept thinking that the author was in my head. Brimming with insights, easily accessible tips and practical advice, this book is the wonderfully strong cup of coffee all parents of multiples need.

"One and the Same: My Life as an Identical Twin and What I've Learned About Everyone's Struggle to Be Singular," Abigail Pobgrebin.
An honest, raw and entertaining look at twinship by American identical twin Pobgrebin, who merges interviews with twins and twin experts with reflections about being inseparable from her twin as a child to experiencing her sister pulling away as an adult.

Notes

1. J.P., "Out of one, many", The Economist, January 12, 2011, https://www.economist.com/blogs/babbage/2011/01/science_singap ore.

2. J.P, "Out of one, many", The Economist, January 12, 2011, https://www.economist.com/blogs/babbage/2011/01/science_singap ore.

3. National Vital Statistics Reports, Vol. 66, No. 1, January 5, 2017, p. 12, https://www.cdc.gov/nchs/data/nvsr/nvsr66/nvsr66_01.pdf

4. Nancy Segal, 2013, "Entwined Lives: Twins and What They Tell Us About Human Behavior," electronic book, Dutton/Plume, p. 362/10666.

5. Nancy Segal, 2013, "Entwined Lives: Twins and What They Tell Us About Human Behavior," electronic book, Dutton/Plume, p. 372/10666.

6. Nancy Segal, 2013, "Entwined Lives: Twins and What They Tell Us About Human Behavior," electronic book, Dutton/Plume, p. 372-412/10666.

7. Nancy Segal, 2013, "Entwined Lives: Twins and What They Tell Us About Human Behavior," electronic book, Dutton/Plume, p. 591/10666.

8. Nancy Segal, 2013, "Entwined Lives: Twins and What They Tell Us About Human Behavior," electronic book, Dutton/Plume, p. 360/10666.

9. Alessandra Piontelli, Twins: From Fetus to Child (Routledge, 2002), 20.

10. Alessandra Piontelli, Twins: From Fetus to Child (Routledge, 2002), 17.

11. Nancy Segal, 2013, "Entwined Lives: Twins and What They Tell Us About Human Behavior," electronic book, Dutton/Plume, p. 372/10666.

12. Alessandra Piontelli, Twins: From Fetus to Child (Routledge, 2002), 18.

13. Nancy Segal, 2013, "Entwined Lives: Twins and What They Tell Us About Human Behavior," electronic book, Dutton/Plume, p. 354/10666.

14. Mary Roach, Spook: Science Tackles the Afterlife (W. W. Norton & Company, 2005,) p. 763-774/3796.

15. Alessandra Piontelli, Twins: From Fetus to Child (Routledge, 2002), 22-26.

16. Alessandra Piontelli, "Twins in utero: temperament development and intertwin behaviour before and after birth" in Twin and Triplet Psychology: A Professional Guide to Working with Multiples, ed. Audrey C Sandbank (London; New York: Routledge, 1999), 12.

17. Jackie Clune, "My triple delight", The Guardian, October 22, 2005, https://www.theguardian.com/lifeandstyle/2005/oct/22/familyandre lationships.family1.

18. Helena Brodtkorb, Mammasjokket. Trøst og oppmuntring for småbarnsmødre (Kagge, 2014)

19. Johanna Grønneberg Mesa, Etter fødselen – det alle glemte å si (Cappelen Damm AS, 2013)

20. Malin Meekatt Birgersson, La mamma bæsje i fred!, (Pantagruel Forlag A/S, 2016)

21. Elin Solvang, "BRUTALT ÆRLIG OM DET STORE MAMMASJOKKET", mamma, August 20, 2014, http://dev.mamma.no/mammaliv/brutalt-%C3%A6rlig-om-det-store-mammasjokket.

22. Jackie Clune, Extreme Motherhood: The Triplet Diaries (Macmillan, 2007), 375.

23. Lars Hveem, "Denne har du fortjent, Bente!", Allers, December 6, 1988.

Lars Hveem/Allers, Letter to Bente Ertresvåg, November 21, 1988.

24. Jackie Clune, Extreme Motherhood: The Triplet Diaries (Macmillan, 2007), 374.

25. "Postnatal depression", NHS, February 11, 2016, https://www.nhs.uk/conditions/post-natal-depression/.

26. Twins Trust study (UK)

27. Linda G. Leonard, "Depression and Anxiety Disorders During Multiple Pregnancy and Parenthood", Journal of Obstetric, Gynecologic, & Neonatal Nursing, 1998, Vol. 27 I, No.3, 329-337. https://doi.org/10.1111/j.1552-6909.1998.tb02656.x. (Info found in abstract in Wiley Online Library: http://onlinelibrary.wiley.com/doi/10.1111/j.1552-6909.1998.tb02656.x/abstract)

28. "Multiple Failings: Parents' of Twins and Triplets Experience of Pre & Post Natal NHS Care", TAMBA UK (now Twins Trust), April 2009.

29. Britta Alin-Åkerman, "The psychology of triplets" in Twin and Triplet Psychology: A Professional Guide to Working with Multiples, ed. Audrey C Sandbank (London; New York: Routledge, 1999), 100.

30. Britta Alin-Åkerman, "The psychology of triplets" in Twin and Triplet Psychology: A Professional Guide to Working with Multiples, ed. Audrey C Sandbank (London; New York: Routledge, 1999), 100.

31. Tamara Eberlein, "What Parents of Multiples Need", Parents, accessed 30 July 2018, http://www.parents.com/baby/twins/raising/what-parents-of-multiples-need/.

32. Barbara Klein, 2012, "Alone in the Mirror: Twins in Therapy," electronic book, Routledge, p. 727/4140, 344/4140.

33. Alessandra Piontelli, Twins: From Fetus to Child (Routledge, 2002), 90.

34. Alessandra Piontelli, Twins: From Fetus to Child (Routledge, 2002), 90.

35. Alessandra Piontelli, Twins: From Fetus to Child (Routledge, 2002), 90.

36. Lars Hveem, "Denne har du fortjent, Bente!", Allers, December 6, 1988.

   Lars Hveem/Allers, Letter to Bente Ertresvåg, November 21, 1988.

37. Lars Hveem, "Denne har du fortjent, Bente!", Allers, December 6, 1988.

   Lars Hveem/Allers, Letter to Bente Ertresvåg, November 21, 1988.

38. Lewis Carroll (1865), Chapter 2: "The Pool of Tears" in *Alice in Wonderland*, available at http://www.literatureproject.com/alice/alice_2.htm

39. Lewis Carroll (1865), Chapter 2: "The Pool of Tears" in *Alice in Wonderland*, available at http://www.literatureproject.com/alice/alice_2.htm.

40. Nancy Segal, 2000, "Entwined Lives: Twins and What They Tell Us About Human Behavior," electronic book, Penguin Group, p. 1951/10666.

41. Nancy Segal, 2000, "Entwined Lives: Twins and What They Tell Us About Human Behavior," electronic book, Penguin Group, p. 1862/10666.

42. Nancy Segal, 2000, "Entwined Lives: Twins and What They Tell Us About Human Behavior," electronic book, Penguin Group, p. 2015/10666.

43. Nancy Segal, 2000, "Entwined Lives: Twins and What They Tell Us About Human Behavior," electronic book, Penguin Group, p. 1862/10666.

44. Heather M. Beauchamp and Lawrence J. Brooks, "The perceptions, policy, and practice of educating twins: a review," Psychology in the schools, 2003, Vol 40(4), 429-438. p.430-431.

45. Barbara Klein, 2012, "Alone in the Mirror: Twins in Therapy," electronic book, Routledge, p. 841/4140.

46. Heather M. Beauchamp and Lawrence J. Brooks, "The perceptions, policy, and practice of educating twins: a review," Psychology in the schools, 2003, Vol 40(4), 429-438. 431.

47. David A. Hay (1999) Adolescent twins and secondary schooling. In: Sandbank AC (ed) Twin and triplet psychology. A professional guide to working with multiples. Routledge, UK, electronic book, p. 2478-2492/4852.

48. Barbara Klein, 2012, "Alone in the Mirror: Twins in Therapy," electronic book, Routledge, p. 841/4140.

49. Heather M. Beauchamp and Lawrence J. Brooks, "The perceptions, policy, and practice of educating twins: a review," Psychology in the schools, 2003, Vol 40(4), 429-438. p.431.

50. Hay & O'Brien (1987) and Hay & O'Brien (1984) quoted in Heather M. Beauchamp and Lawrence J. Brooks, "The perceptions, policy, and practice of educating twins: a review," Psychology in the schools, 2003, Vol 40(4), 429-438. p 431.

51. Anne Bruce study quoted in David A. Hay (1999) Adolescent twins and secondary schooling. In: Sandbank AC (ed) Twin and triplet psychology. A professional guide to working with multiples. Routledge, UK, electronic book, p. 2721-2734/4852.

52. David A. Hay (1999) Adolescent twins and secondary schooling. In: Sandbank AC (ed) Twin and triplet psychology. A professional guide to working with multiples. Routledge, UK, electronic book, p. 2721/4852.

53. Hay & O'Brien, 1987 and Hay & O'Brien, 1984 quoted in Heather M. Beauchamp and Lawrence J. Brooks, "The perceptions, policy, and practice of educating twins: a review," Psychology in the schools, 2003, Vol 40(4), 429-438. p 431.

54. Anne Bruce study quoted in David A. Hay (1999) Adolescent twins and secondary schooling. In: Sandbank AC (ed) Twin and triplet psychology. A professional guide to working with multiples. Routledge, UK, electronic book, p. 2721-2734/4852.

55. Anne Bruce study quoted in David A. Hay (1999) Adolescent twins and secondary schooling. In: Sandbank AC (ed) Twin and triplet psychology. A professional guide to working with multiples. Routledge, UK, electronic book, p. 2721-2734/4852.

56. Anne Bruce study quoted in David A. Hay (1999) Adolescent twins and secondary schooling. In: Sandbank AC (ed) Twin and triplet psychology. A professional guide to working with multiples. Routledge, UK, electronic book, p. 2721-2734/4852.

57. Gleeson et al. (1990) (https://www.ncbi.nlm.nih.gov/pubmed/2239109) quoted in Hay (1999) quoted in Heather M. Beauchamp and Lawrence J. Brooks, "The perceptions, policy, and practice of educating twins: a review," Psychology in the schools, 2003, Vol 40(4), 429-438. p 431.

58. Varpu Penninkilampi-Kerola. 'IMPLICATIONS OF CO-TWIN DEPENDENCE FOR TWINS' SOCIAL INTERACTIONS, MENTAL HEALTH AND ALCOHOL USE: A follow-up study of Finnish twins from adolescence to early adulthood, PhD University of Helsinki, p.18.

59. Alessandra Piontelli, Twins: From Fetus to Child (Routledge, 2002), 130.

60. Alessandra Piontelli, Twins: From Fetus to Child (Routledge, 2002), 131.

61. Alessandra Piontelli, Twins: From Fetus to Child (Routledge, 2002), 131.

62. Joan A. Friedman, 2008, "Emotionally Healthy Twins: A New Philosophy for Parenting Two Unique Children", electronic book, Da Capo Lifelong Books, p. 755/3830.

63. Joan A. Friedman, 2008, "Emotionally Healthy Twins: A New Philosophy for Parenting Two Unique Children", electronic book, Da Capo Lifelong Books, p. 802/3830.

64. Lewis Carroll, Alice in Wonderland, Day 4 of 29, available at http://www.turtlereader.com/authors/lewis-carroll/alices-adventures-in-wonderland-day-4-of-29/.

65. Dorothy Burlingham, "The Fantasy of Having a Twin", Psychoanalytic Study of the Child 1 (1945): 205–210, quoted in David Greenberg and Maida Greenberg, "Dorothy Burlingham's Twins", Slate, August 25, 2011, http://www.slate.com/articles/life/twins/2011/08/dorothy_burlingh ams_twins.html?via=gdpr-consent.

66. Dorothy Burlingham, "The Fantasy of Having a Twin", Psychoanalytic Study of the Child 1 (1945): 205–210, quoted in David Greenberg and Maida Greenberg, "Dorothy Burlingham's Twins", Slate, August 25, 2011, http://www.slate.com/articles/life/twins/2011/08/dorothy_burlingh ams_twins.html?via=gdpr-consent.

67. Dionne Searcey, "At a Convention Full of Them, It's Apparent Not All Twins Are Created Equal", The Wall Street Journal, August 9, 2011, https://www.wsj.com/articles/SB10001424053111904140604576496073 704987498.

68. Jenny Brockie (2006). Two of a kind. Insight (Television program), SBS-TV, quoted on Trove National Library of Australia, https://trove.nla.gov.au/work/19625833?selectedversion=NBD409963 78 & "Two of a Kind", SBS TV, accessed 30 July 2018, https://www.sbs.com.au/news/insight/tvepisode/

69. Abigail Pobgrebin, 2009, "One and the same: My Life as an Identical Twin and What I've Learned about Everyone's Struggle to Be Singular", electronic book, Anchor, p. 175-191/5079.

70. Abigail Pobgrebin, 2009, "One and the same: My Life as an Identical Twin and What I've Learned about Everyone's Struggle to Be Singular", electronic book, Anchor, p. 175-191/5079.

71. Tatiana Morales, "The Life Of Identical Triplets…", CBS News, March 31, 2004, https://www.cbsnews.com/news/the-life-of-identical-triplets/.

72. Emine Saner, "Life after Harry Potter", The Guardian, July 2, 2011, https://www.theguardian.com/lifeandstyle/2011/jul/02/harry-potter-james-oliver-phelps-weasley-twins.

73. Emine Saner, "Life after Harry Potter", The Guardian, July 2, 2011, https://www.theguardian.com/lifeandstyle/2011/jul/02/harry-potter-james-oliver-phelps-weasley-twins.

74. Emine Saner, "Life after Harry Potter", The Guardian, July 2, 2011, https://www.theguardian.com/lifeandstyle/2011/jul/02/harry-potter-james-oliver-phelps-weasley-twins.

75. Julia Felsenthal, *Three Identical Strangers* Revisits a Shadowy Scientific Conspiracy", VOGUE, June 29, 2018, https://www.vogue.com/article/three-identical-strangers-documentary-tim-wardle-movie-review.

76. Sara Stewart, "Separated-at-birth triplets met tragic end after shocking psych experiment", New York Post, June 23, 2018, https://nypost.com/2018/06/23/these-triplets-were-separated-at-birth-for-a-twisted-psych-study/.

77. Julia Felsenthal, "Three Identical Strangers Revisits a Shadowy Scientific Conspiracy", VOGUE, June 29, 2018, https://www.vogue.com/article/three-identical-strangers-documentary-tim-wardle-movie-review.

78. Jake Nevins, "Three Identical Strangers: the bizarre tale of triplets separated at birth", The Guardian, June 28, 2018, https://www.theguardian.com/film/2018/jun/28/three-identical-strangers-the-bizarre-tale-of-triplets-separated-at-birth.

79. Jake Nevins, "Three Identical Strangers: the bizarre tale of triplets separated at birth", The Guardian, June 28, 2018, https://www.theguardian.com/film/2018/jun/28/three-identical-strangers-the-bizarre-tale-of-triplets-separated-at-birth.

80. Gregory Wakeman, "Are the 'Three Identical Strangers' brothers still close? Here's what its director told us", metro, July 3, 2018, https://www.metro.us/entertainment/movies/are-the-three-identical-strangers-brothers-still-close.

81. Gregory Wakeman, "Are the 'Three Identical Strangers' brothers still close? Here's what its director told us", metro, July 3, 2018, https://www.metro.us/entertainment/movies/are-the-three-identical-strangers-brothers-still-close.

82. Emily Nussbaum, "Sliding Doors, nymag.com, October 14, 2017, http://nymag.com/arts/books/features/39290/.

83. Barbara Klein, Not All Twins Are Alike: Psychological Profiles of Twinship (Praeger, 2003), p.104.

84. Dorothy Burlingham, "The Fantasy of Having a Twin", Psychoanalytic Study of the Child 1 (1945): 205–210, quoted in David Greenberg and Maida Greenberg, "Dorothy Burlingham's Twins", Slate, August 25, 2011, http://www.slate.com/articles/life/twins/2011/08/dorothy_burlinghams_twins.html?via=gdpr-consent.

85. Pat Preedy, "Meeting the educational needs of pre-school and primary aged twins and higher multiples" in Twin and Triplet Psychology: A Professional Guide to Working with Multiples' edited by Audrey Sandbank,1999. Routledge. electronic book, p. 1777/4852.

86. Pat Preedy, "Meeting the educational needs of pre-school and primary aged twins and higher multiples" in Twin and Triplet Psychology: A Professional Guide to Working with Multiples' edited by Audrey Sandbank,1999. Routledge. electronic book, p. 1777/4852.

87. Alessandra Piontelli, Twins: From Fetus to Child (Routledge, 2002), 114.

88. Alessandra Piontelli, Twins: From Fetus to Child (Routledge, 2002), 116.

89. "The Gestalt Principles", Graphic Design at Spokane Falls Community College, accessed August 8, 2018, http://graphicdesign.spokanefalls.edu/tutorials/process/gestaltprinciples/gestaltprinc.htm.

90. Alessandra Piontelli, Twins: From Fetus to Child (Routledge, 2002), 116.

91. Alessandra Piontelli, Twins: From Fetus to Child (Routledge, 2002), 116.

92. Barbara Klein, 2012, "Alone in the Mirror: Twins in Therapy," electronic book, Routledge, p. 1041/4140.

93. Barbara Klein, 2012, "Alone in the Mirror: Twins in Therapy," electronic book, Routledge, p. 1043/4140.

94. Barbara Klein, 2012, "Alone in the Mirror: Twins in Therapy," electronic book, Routledge, p. 1043/4140.

95. Barbara Klein, Not All Twins Are Alike: Psychological Profiles of Twinship (Praeger, 2003), p13.

96. Barbara Klein, Not All Twins Are Alike: Psychological Profiles of Twinship (Praeger, 2003), p.13.

97. Christina Baglivi Tinglof, "Will Too Much Togetherness Affect Your Twins' Individuation?", Talk About Twins [blog], accessed March 12, 2018, http://christinabaglivitinglof.com/school-age-twins/will-too-much-togetherness-affect-your-twins-individuation/.

98. Faiza Elmasry, "Same but Different: Twins Face Double Challenges", VOA News, February 11, 2014, https://www.voanews.com/a/same-but-different-twins-face-double-challenges/1848947.html

99. Karen Thorpe and Karen Gardner, "Twins and Their Friendships: Differences Between Monozygotic, Dizygotic Same-Sex and Dizygotic Mixed-Sex Pairs", Twin Research and Human Genetics (March 2006): 155. DOI: 10.1375/183242706776402984.

100. Barbara Klein, 2012, "Alone in the Mirror: Twins in Therapy," electronic book, Routledge, p. 3298/4140.

101. Karen Thorpe and Karen Gardner, "Twins and Their Friendships: Differences Between Monozygotic, Dizygotic Same-Sex and Dizygotic Mixed-Sex Pairs", Twin Research and Human Genetics (March 2006): 155. DOI: 10.1375/183242706776402984.

102. Nancy Segal, 2000 "Entwined Lives: Twins and What They Tell Us About Human Behavior", electronic book, Penguin Group, p. 2487/10666.

103. Christina Baglivi Tinglof, "Will Too Much Togetherness Affect Your Twins' Individuation?", Talk About Twins [blog], accessed March 12, 2018, http://christinabaglivitinglof.com/school-age-twins/will-too-much-togetherness-affect-your-twins-individuation/.

104. Joan A. Friedman, 'The Scrooge of Twindom' https://www.joanafriedmanphd.com/the-scrooge-of-twindom-2/

105. Carol Cooper, Twins & Multiple Births: The essential parenting guide from pregnancy to adulthood, (Random House, 1997), 231.

106. Faiza Elmasry, "Same but Different: Twins Face Double Challenges", VOA News, February 11, 2014, https://www.voanews.com/a/same-but-different-twins-face-double-challenges/1848947.html.

107. Britta Alin-Åkerman, "The psychology of triplets" in Twin and Triplet Psychology: A Professional Guide to Working with Multiples, ed. Audrey C Sandbank (London; New York: Routledge, 1999), 100.

108. Karen Thorpe and Karen Gardner. "Twins and Their Friendships: Differences Between Monozygotic, Dizygotic Same-Sex and Dizygotic Mixed-Sex Pairs," Twin Res Hum Genet. 2006 Feb;9(1):155-64. (Link: https://www.ncbi.nlm.nih.gov/pubmed/16611481)

109. Karen Thorpe and Karen Gardner. "Twins and Their Friendships: Differences Between Monozygotic, Dizygotic Same-Sex and Dizygotic Mixed-Sex Pairs," Twin Res Hum Genet. 2006 Feb;9(1):155-64. (Link: https://www.ncbi.nlm.nih.gov/pubmed/16611481)

110. Pat Preedy, 2001, "Are multiple birth children different from singletons? Meeting the educational needs of multiple birth children upon school entry." Unpublished doctoral dissertation, University of Birmingham, UK, quoted in Karen Thorpe and Karen Gardner. "Twins and Their Friendships: Differences Between Monozygotic, Dizygotic Same-Sex and Dizygotic Mixed-Sex Pairs," Twin Res Hum Genet. 2006 Feb;9(1):155-64. p.155.

111. Karen Thorpe and Karen Gardner. "Twins and Their Friendships: Differences Between Monozygotic, Dizygotic Same-Sex and Dizygotic Mixed-Sex Pairs," Twin Res Hum Genet. 2006 Feb;9(1):155-64. p.155.

112. Karen Thorpe and Karen Gardner. "Twins and Their Friendships: Differences Between Monozygotic, Dizygotic Same-Sex and Dizygotic Mixed-Sex Pairs," Twin Res Hum Genet. 2006 Feb;9(1):155-64. p.155.

113. Jay Joseph, "The Use of the Classical Twin Method in the Social and Behavioral Sciences: The Fallacy Continues" The Journal of Mind and Behavior, 2013, Vol. 34 (1), 1–39. p. 2.

114. Jay Joseph, "The Use of the Classical Twin Method in the Social and Behavioral Sciences: The Fallacy Continues" The Journal of Mind and Behavior, 2013, Vol. 34 (1), 1–39. p. 2

115. Karen Thorpe and Karen Gardner. "Twins and Their Friendships: Differences Between Monozygotic, Dizygotic Same-Sex and Dizygotic Mixed-Sex Pairs," Twin Res Hum Genet. 2006 Feb;9(1):155-64. p.161.

116. "Malaysian twins spared death row", BBC News, February 7, 2009, http://news.bbc.co.uk/1/hi/world/asia-pacific/7876221.stm.

117. Brian Palmer, "Can Identical Twins Get Away With Murder?", Slate, August 23, 2014, http://www.slate.com/articles/news_and_politics/explainer/2012/08/true_crime_with_twins_can_identical_twins_get_away_with_murder_.html.

118. Genetic Science Learning Center. What is Cloning. Retrieved August 11, 2018, from https://learn.genetics.utah.edu/content/cloning/whatiscloning/

119. "What is cloning", 'Biotechnology' Facebook page, April 4, 2011, https://www.facebook.com/174999342548268/photos/a.178048445576 691.36798.174999342548268/178048712243331/?type=3

120. "Cloning Activity – My eCoach", my eCoach, retrieved August 11, 2018, https://my-ecoach.com/online/resources/6661/Cloning_Activity_(Day_22).doc

121. Ajay Dasgupta, "What is Cloning?", Pitara Kids Network, retrieved August 11, 2018, https://www.pitara.com/science-for-kids/5ws-and-h/what-is-cloning/.

122. Genetic Science Learning Center. What is Cloning. Retrieved August 11, 2018, from https://learn.genetics.utah.edu/content/cloning/whatiscloning/

123. Nancy Segal, 2000 "Entwined Lives: Twins and What They Tell Us About Human Behavior," electronic book, Penguin Group, p. 651/10666.

124. Nancy Segal, 2000 "Entwined Lives: Twins and What They Tell Us About Human Behavior," electronic book, Penguin Group, p. 661/10666.

125. Genetic Science Learning Center. (2013, July 15) Insights From Identical Twins. Retrieved August 10, 2018, from https://learn.genetics.utah.edu/content/epigenetics/twins/.

126. Genetic Science Learning Center. (2013, July 15) Insights From Identical Twins. Retrieved August 10, 2018, from https://learn.genetics.utah.edu/content/epigenetics/twins/.

127. Genetic Science Learning Center. (2016, March 1) What are DNA and Genes?. Retrieved August 10, 2018, from https://learn.genetics.utah.edu/content/basics/dna.

128. Genetic Science Learning Center. (2013, July 15) Insights From Identical Twins. Retrieved August 10, 2018, from https://learn.genetics.utah.edu/content/epigenetics/twins/

129. Genetic Science Learning Center. (2013, July 15) Insights From Identical Twins. Retrieved August 10, 2018, from https://learn.genetics.utah.edu/content/epigenetics/twins/.

130. Genetic Science Learning Center. (2013, July 15) Insights From Identical Twins. Retrieved August 10, 2018, from https://learn.genetics.utah.edu/content/epigenetics/twins/.

131. Genetic Science Learning Center. (2013, July 15) Insights From Identical Twins. Retrieved August 10, 2018, from https://learn.genetics.utah.edu/content/epigenetics/twins/

132. Genetic Science Learning Center. (2013, July 15) Insights From Identical Twins. Retrieved August 10, 2018, from https://learn.genetics.utah.edu/content/epigenetics/twins/.

133. Lone Frank (2011), My Beautiful Genome: Exposing Our Genetic Future, One Quirk at a Time (Oneworld Publications), p. 235.

134. Chris Pummer, "Will the baby look like you?", Considerable, June 2, 2008, https://considerable.com/will-the-baby-look-like-you/.

135. Chris Pummer, "Will the baby look like you?", Considerable, June 2, 2008, https://considerable.com/will-the-baby-look-like-you/.

136. Anne Matthews, "Re: Epigenetics, baking cakes and quote or background for a book?" Message to Kari Ertresvåg, May 16, 2017, Email.

137. Graham Pike, "Re: Question re facial recognition for book on twins and triplets" Message to Kari Ertresvåg, April 9, 2017, Email.

138. David A. Hay (1999) Adolescent twins and secondary schooling. In: Sandbank AC (ed) Twin and triplet psychology. A professional guide to working with multiples. Routledge, UK, electronic book, p. 2547/4852.

139. David A. Hay (1999) Adolescent twins and secondary schooling. In: Sandbank AC (ed) Twin and triplet psychology. A professional guide to working with multiples. Routledge, UK, electronic book, p. 2805/4852.

140. Barbara Klein, Not All Twins Are Alike: Psychological Profiles of Twinship (Praeger, 2003), 36.

141. Barbara Klein, Not All Twins Are Alike: Psychological Profiles of Twinship (Praeger, 2003), 14-15.

142. Bullying and Victimization: The Effect of Close Companionship, https://www.cambridge.org/core/journals/twin-research-and-human-genetics/article/bullying-and-victimization-the-effect-of-close-companionship/38789B15793DA0D2A5019C2FBB14EC8E/core-reader

143. Bullying and Victimization: The Effect of Close Companionship, https://www.cambridge.org/core/journals/twin-research-and-human-genetics/article/bullying-and-victimization-the-effect-of-close-companionship/38789B15793DA0D2A5019C2FBB14EC8E/core-reader

144. Britta Alin-Åkerman 1999, "The psychology of triplets" in 'Twin and Triplet Psychology: A Professional Guide to Working With Multiples', edited by Audrey C. Sandbank, electronic book, Routledge.p. 2334/4852.

145. "Twin Bullying", reddit, accessed 10 August 2018, https://www.reddit.com/r/Twins/comments/3twr4w/twin_bullying/.

146. Sara Pascoe, Animal: The Autobiography of a Female Body (Faber & Faber, 2016), 209.

147. Barbara Klein, Not All Twins Are Alike: Psychological Profiles of Twinship (Praeger, 2003), 38.

148. Heather M. Beauchamp and Lawrence J. Brooks, "The perceptions, policy, and practice of educating twins: a review," Psychology in the schools, 2003, Vol 40(4), 429-438. p.429.

149. "Twins in school – together or apart?", BBC, August 28, 2001, http://news.bbc.co.uk/2/hi/uk_news/education/1480297.stm.

150. Heather M. Beauchamp Lawrence J. Brooks Jr., "The perceptions, policy, and practice of educating twins: A review ", Psychology in the Schools, Vol. 40(4), 2003, Pages 429-438. p.429.

151. Ginia Bellafante, "Born Together, Raised Together, So Why Not in Classroom, Too?", The New York Times, February 24, 2006, http://www.nytimes.com/2006/02/24/us/born-together-raised-together-so-why-not-in-classroom-too.html.

152. Joan A. Friedman, "Twins Sharing Friends", accessed 10 December 2017, https://www.joanafriedmanphd.com/twins-sharing-friends/.

153. Judy W. Hagedorn and Janet W. Kizziar, Gemini: The psychology and phenomena of twin (Droke House/Hallux 1974), p 97-98.

154. David A. Hay, "Adolescent twins and secondary schooling" in Twin and Triplet Psychology: A Professional Guide to Working with Multiples, ed. Audrey C Sandbank (London; New York: Routledge, 1999),129.

155. David A. Hay, "Adolescent twins and secondary schooling" in Twin and Triplet Psychology: A Professional Guide to Working with Multiples, ed. Audrey C Sandbank (London; New York: Routledge, 1999), 129.

156. Webpage no longer available. Comment left by Felisa J Vázquez-Abad)

157. David A. Hay, "Adolescent twins and secondary schooling" in Twin and Triplet Psychology: A Professional Guide to Working with Multiples, ed. Audrey C Sandbank (London; New York: Routledge, 1999), 129.

158. David A. Hay (1999) Adolescent twins and secondary schooling. In: Sandbank AC (ed) Twin and triplet psychology. A professional guide to working with multiples. Routledge, UK, electronic book, p. 2691/4852.

159. Barbara Klein, 2012, "Alone in the Mirror: Twins in Therapy," electronic book, Routledge, p. 512/4140.

160. Barbara Klein, 2012, "Alone in the Mirror: Twins in Therapy," electronic book, Routledge, p. 2282/4140.

161. Barbara Klein, 2012, "Alone in the Mirror: Twins in Therapy," electronic book, Routledge, p. 568/4140.

162. Joan A. Friedman, Two Peas in a Pod: An Imprecise Science, https://www.joanafriedmanphd.com/two-peas-in-a-pod-an-imprecise-science/?fbclid=IwAR2jQXuDHqQGkbGMlEKF9KQ5SfRrUuZxaJbqEjV vp1lFzo3_7Nl2WsBENwg, accessed 28 June 2019.

163. Joan A. Friedman, Two Peas in a Pod: An Imprecise Science, https://www.joanafriedmanphd.com/two-peas-in-a-pod-an-imprecise-science/?fbclid=IwAR2jQXuDHqQGkbGMlEKF9KQ5SfRrUuZxaJbqEjV vp1lFzo3_7Nl2WsBENwg, accessed 28 June 2019.

164. "Anorexic Twins May Hold Cure to Eating Disorders", ABC News, March 17, 2007, http://abcnews.go.com/GMA/OnCall/story?id=2959592&page=1.

165. "Is Anorexia in the Genes? Twin Studies Offer Clues", The Washington Post, February 16, 1998, http://articles.latimes.com/1998/feb/16/health/he-19687.

166. Anna Goodman, Amy Heshmati, Ninoa Malki, Ilona Koupil; Associations Between Birth Characteristics and Eating Disorders Across the Life Course: Findings From 2 Million Males and Females Born in Sweden, 1975–1998, American Journal of Epidemiology, Volume 179, Issue 7, April 1 2014, p. 852–863, https://doi.org/10.1093/aje/kwt445.

167. Debra M. Cooper, "Twin Studies Reveal Eating Disorder Connection", Eating Disorder Hope, January 4, 2016, https://www.eatingdisorderhope.com/blog/twin-studies-reveal-eating-disorder-connection.

168. Keel, P. K., & Forney, K. J. (2013). Psychosocial risk factors for eating disorders. Int J Eat Disord, 46(5), 433-439. doi:10.1002/eat.22094. quoted in "Risiko- og sårbarhetsfaktorer ved spiseforstyrrelser", Helsedirektoratet, accessed August 20, 2017, https://helsedirektoratet.no/retningslinjer/spiseforstyrrelser/seksjon? Tittel=risiko-og-sarbarhetsfaktorer-ved-10512.

169. "Anorexic Twins May Hold Cure to Eating Disorders", ABC News, March 17, 2007, http://abcnews.go.com/GMA/OnCall/story?id=2959592&page=1.

170. "A Day In The Life Of Identical Twins With Identical Eating Disorders", Huffpost, October 12, 2016 https://www.huffingtonpost.com/entry/day-in-life-of-identical-twins-with-eating-disorders_us_57fdeacee4b0d505a46b0e69

171. 'Foreldrerådet' Kroppspress med barnepsykolog Elisabeth Gerhardsen, https://www.acast.com/foreldreradet/kroppspressmedbarnepsykolog elisabethgerhardsen, September 26, 2016, 06:45-07.40.

172. Stef Daniel, "Dare to Compare: Raising Twins to Be Themselves", accessed 10 August 2018, https://www.everydayfamily.com/raising-twins-to-be-themselves/.

173. "Parental Worries and Challenges", Twins List, accessed August 12, 2018, http://www.twinslist.org/sibling2.htm#frustrations.

174. Audrey C. Sandbank 1999, "Personality, identity and family relationships" in 'Twin and Triplet Psychology: A Professional Guide to Working With Multiples', edited by Audrey C. Sandbank, electronic book, Routledge. p. 3526/4852.

175. Nadine Brozan, "Relationships: The impact of twins on siblings", The New York Times, February 22, 1982, https://www.nytimes.com/1982/02/22/style/relationships-the-impact-of-twins-on-siblings.html.

176. "Older siblings" in Twins and Multiples, Curtin University, accessed 8 August 2018, http://tandm.curtin.edu.au/preschool/p1b.cfm.

177. "Parental Worries and Challenges", Twins List, accessed August 12, 2018, http://www.twinslist.org/sibling2.htm#frustrations.

178. Audrey C. Sandbank 1999, "Personality, identity and family relationships" in 'Twin and Triplet Psychology: A Professional Guide to Working With Multiples', edited by Audrey C. Sandbank, electronic book, Routledge. p. 3507/4852.

179. Nadine Brozan, "Relationships: The impact of twins on siblings", The New York Times, February 22, 1982, https://www.nytimes.com/1982/02/22/style/relationships-the-impact-of-twins-on-siblings.html.

180. Britta Alin-Åkerman, "The psychology of triplets" in 'Twin and Triplet Psychology: A Professional Guide to Working With Multiples', edited by Audrey C. Sandbank. 1999. Routledge. Electronic book, p 2300/4852, p. 2337/4852.

181. Frank J. Sulloway, Born to Rebel, quoted in Frank J. Sulloway, Ph.D, ">Born to Rebel", Sulloway.org, accessed 8 August 2018, http://www.sulloway.org/borntorebel.html.

182. Pat Preedy, "Meeting the educational needs of pre-school and primary aged twins and higher multiples" in Twin and Triplet Psychology: A Professional Guide to Working with Multiples, ed. Audrey C Sandbank (London; New York: Routledge, 1999), 67.

183. "TWINS STUDY", NASA, accessed July 1, 2018, https://www.nasa.gov/twins-study

184. Alessandra Potenza and Loren Grush, "Astronauts Scott and Mark Kelly on NASA's twin experiment and the future of space travel", The Verge, March 21, 2017, https://www.theverge.com/2017/3/21/14805232/nasa-twin-study-astronauts-mark-scott-kelly-space-interview.

185. Lizzie Pook, "I've never needed anyone else': life as an identical twin", The Guardian, October 29, 2016 https://www.theguardian.com/lifeandstyle/2016/oct/29/identical-twin-never-needed-anyone-else.

186. Lizzie Pook, "I've never needed anyone else': life as an identical twin", The Guardian, October 29, 2016 https://www.theguardian.com/lifeandstyle/2016/oct/29/identical-twin-never-needed-anyone-else.

187. Rene Zazzo, "The twin condition and the couple effects on personality development.", Acta geneticae medicae et gemellologiae: twin research (1976). https://doi.org/10.1017/S0001566000014409.

188. David A. Hay (1999) Adolescent twins and secondary schooling. In: Sandbank AC (ed) Twin and triplet psychology. A professional guide to working with multiples. Routledge, UK, electronic book, p. 2855/4852.

189. Alessandra Piontelli, Twins: From Fetus to Child (Routledge, 2012), 116.

190. Abigail Pobgrebin, 2009, "One and the same: My Life as an Identical Twin and What I've Learned about Everyone's Struggle to Be Singular", electronic book, Anchor, p. 47/5079.

191. Abigail Pobgrebin, 2009, "One and the same: My Life as an Identical Twin and What I've Learned about Everyone's Struggle to Be Singular", electronic book, Anchor, p. 1373/5079.

192. Abigail Pobgrebin, 2009, "One and the same: My Life as an Identical Twin and What I've Learned about Everyone's Struggle to Be Singular", electronic book, Anchor, p. 2778/5079.

193. Lizzie Pook, "I've never needed anyone else': life as an identical twin", The Guardian, October 29, 2016 https://www.theguardian.com/lifeandstyle/2016/oct/29/identical-twin-never-needed-anyone-else

194. Barbara Klein, 2012, "Alone in the Mirror: Twins in Therapy," electronic book, Routledge, p. 841/4140.

195. Abigail Pobgrebin, 2009, "One and the same: My Life as an Identical Twin and What I've Learned about Everyone's Struggle to Be Singular", electronic book, Anchor, p. 948/5079.

196. Veronica Hefner & Barbara J. Wilson, "From Love at First Sight to Soul Mate: The Influence of Romantic Ideals in Popular Films on Young People's Beliefs about Relationships," Communication Monographs, (2013):4. DOI:10.1080/03637751.2013.776697, p.4.

197. Sandra L. Murray, John G. Holmes, Dale W. Griffin, "The Self-Fulfilling Nature of Positive Illusions in Romantic Relationships: Love Is Not Blind, but Prescient", Journal of Personality and Social Psychology, 1996, Vol. 7 I, No. 6, 1155-1180 http://citeseerx.ist.psu.edu/viewdoc/download?doi=10.1.1.590.473&rep=rep1&type=pdf.

198. Sandra L. Murray, John G. Holmes, Dale W. Griffin, "The Self-Fulfilling Nature of Positive Illusions in Romantic Relationships: Love Is Not Blind, but Prescient", Journal of Personality and Social Psychology, 1996, Vol. 7 I, No. 6, 1155-1180. http://citeseerx.ist.psu.edu/viewdoc/download?doi=10.1.1.590.473&rep=rep1&type=pdf.

199. Barbara Klein, Not All Twins Are Alike: Psychological Profiles of Twinship (Praeger, 2003), 54.

200. "Am Married To A Twin", Experience Project, http://www.experienceproject.com/stories/Am-Married-To-A-Twin/1094470 [site is suspended; https://en.wikipedia.org/wiki/Experience_Project]

201. "Am Married To A Twin", Experience Project, http://www.experienceproject.com/stories/Am-Married-To-A-Twin/1094470 [site is suspended; https://en.wikipedia.org/wiki/Experience_Project]

202. "Am Married To A Twin", Experience Project, http://www.experienceproject.com/stories/Am-Married-To-A-Twin/1094470 [site is suspended; https://en.wikipedia.org/wiki/Experience_Project]

203. Barbara Klein, 2012, "Alone in the Mirror: Twins in Therapy," electronic book, Routledge, p. 2562/4140.

204. Sophie Cassell (2011). Examining the Twin Bond: A look at the psychological development of twins and the differences in individuality and identity differentiation between fraternal and identical same-sex twins. American University. [https://auislandora.wrlc.org/islandora/object/1011capstones:161/datastream/PDF/view]

205. Barbara Klein, 2012, "Alone in the Mirror: Twins in Therapy," electronic book, Routledge, p. 673/4140.

206. Audrey C Sandbank, "Personality, identity and family relationships" in Twin and Triplet Psychology: A Professional Guide to Working with Multiples, ed. Audrey C Sandbank (London; New York: Routledge, 1999), 152.

207. "Exclusively Twins", Twins Realm, accessed July 1, 2018, http://www.twinsrealm.com/dating2.htm.

208. Katy Winter, "Time for a break? The twins who decided it was finally time to live by themselves... after NINETY years together", Mail Online, September 9, 2014, http://www.dailymail.co.uk/femail/article-2747613/Time-break-96-year-old-twins-spent-lives-decide-s-finally-time-homes.html.

209. Katy Winter, "Time for a break? The twins who decided it was finally time to live by themselves... after NINETY years together", Mail Online, September 9, 2014, http://www.dailymail.co.uk/femail/article-2747613/Time-break-96-year-old-twins-spent-lives-decide-s-finally-time-homes.html.

210. Katy Winter, "Time for a break? The twins who decided it was finally time to live by themselves... after NINETY years together", Mail Online, September 9, 2014, http://www.dailymail.co.uk/femail/article-2747613/Time-break-96-year-old-twins-spent-lives-decide-s-finally-time-homes.html.

211. David J. Sharrow and James J. Anderson (2016), A Twin Protection Effect? Explaining Twin Survival Advantages with a Two-Process Mortality Model. PLoS ONE 11(5): e0154774. https://doi.org/10.1371/journal.pone.0154774, quoted in Alyssa Braithwaite, "Twins live longer, a new study has found", SBS, July 21, 2017, https://www.sbs.com.au/topics/life/health/article/2016/08/19/twins-live-longer-new-study-has-found.

212. David J. Sharrow and James J. Anderson (2016), A Twin Protection Effect? Explaining Twin Survival Advantages with a Two-Process Mortality Model. PLoS ONE 11(5): e0154774. https://doi.org/10.1371/journal.pone.0154774, quoted in Alyssa Braithwaite, "Twins live longer, a new study has found", SBS, July 21, 2017, https://www.sbs.com.au/topics/life/health/article/2016/08/19/twins-live-longer-new-study-has-found.

213. David Greenberg and Maida Greenberg, "Dorothy Burlingham's Twins", SLATE, August 25, 2011, http://www.slate.com/articles/life/twins/2011/08/dorothy_burlinghams_twins.html?via=gdpr-consent.

Printed in Great Britain
by Amazon